P9-ELR-742

Learning Made Easy

ENGLISH
Made Easy

pil

Publications International, Ltd.

Contributing writers:
Susan Bloom is a freelance writer and editor with Creative Services Associates, Inc., a publisher of educational materials. She has taught composition and literature at a community college for 15 years. She holds a B.S. in English from Southern Methodist University and an M.A. in English from the University of California–Los Angeles.

Flora Foss is a writer and editor with Creative Services Associates, Inc. She has taught language arts and science to middle school students, literature and writing to junior college students, and poetry writing to students of all ages. She received a B.S. in Education in Biology and an M.A. in Literature from Northern Illinois University in DeKalb, Illinois.

Maggie Ronzani is a writer and editor with Creative Services Associates, Inc. She has more than 25 years of experience in educational publishing. She has an A.B. in English from Creighton University in Omaha and an M.B.A. in Marketing from DePaul University in Chicago.

Consultant:
Dorothy F. King, Ed.D., is a consultant in language and literacy and has served as Chair for the National Council of Teachers of English Commission on Curriculum.

Cover illustration: Garry Colby
Illustrations: Garry Colby, Rémy Simard

CONTENTS

English and You

You already know how to use the English language. After all, you speak, read, and write English. Yet everyone needs help with homework sometimes, and *English Made Easy* can help you when you run into a problem. You'll find information about grammar that you can use whenever you think you need it. This book is a handy reference to pick up when you are completing assignments for English or any topic that requires writing.

English Made Easy was prepared with the help of educational specialists. It offers quick, simple explanations of the basic material you're studying in school. If you get stuck on an idea or have trouble finding some information, this study reference can help solve it for you. It can also help your parents assist you by giving them a refresher course on the subject.

The dialect used in this book is Standard English. *Dialect* is a regional variety of a language. There are many dialects in English. Everyone uses a dialect, and no dialect is wrong. But Standard English has one major advantage: It is the dialect used by people with political, economic, and social power. By learning Standard English, you increase your own possibilities for success in society.

Grammar

The main point of language is to communicate meaning. A person is judged by his or her skill at doing this in speech or writing. Grammar is one method of getting your meaning across. Grammar describes the way the English language works. When you use grammar correctly, you communicate your thoughts clearly, and people understand you.

English Made Easy covers sentences and parts of speech, the basic building blocks of the English language. It also explains the rules governing capitalization and punctuation in English. Like a dictionary or thesaurus, this book is meant to be one of many reference tools available to you—a tool that you decide when and how to use.

Using this Book

English Made Easy is organized by the topics you'll be studying in English. The Table of Contents shows which chapter covers the topic you're working on. For more help finding what you need to know, use the Index to look up key words related to what you're studying. You may find material faster this way. Also, use the laminated "Keys to Grammar Quick Study Card." It's designed to be kept in a three-ring notebook for quick-look answers to common questions.

Every chapter of *English Made Easy* offers lots of fun quizzes and games so you can test yourself on what you've been learning. It is not a write-in workbook, so keep paper handy for writing your answers. You can check your answers in the "Answers" section at the end of each chapter.

Different teachers and schools take different approaches to teaching English. For this reason, we recommend that you talk with your teacher about using *English Made Easy.* You might even let your teacher look through this book so he or she can help you use it in a way that best matches the topics you're studying at school.

Sentences
Express Complete Thoughts!

What is always "sent" when you say or ask something?
A sentence! A sentence tells other people a complete thought
or idea you want them to know.

What Is a Sentence?

A sentence joins words together. Also, a sentence can be just one word, like "Yes!" In this case, the person getting the message knows what you mean even though you aren't saying it. The person knows you mean "Yes! I agree with you," for example. A sentence can be two or three words, such as "Stop now!" or "On the table." Again, the message receiver knows the situation and you don't have to say all the words for the person to get the meaning. But these sentences are special cases. What if the person doesn't know the situation? You need to use sentences that give the person all the information needed so she or he can make sense of your message.

A sentence gives words more meaning. Look at these words:

an angry black cloud dust funnel huge in of the swirled

DUST THE
AN BLACK
FUNNEL
ANGRY CLOUD IN
HUGE SWIRLED
OF

The words do not make much sense. How can you fix this? You can make a sentence! Sentences put words together so they make sense. Sentences form a complete thought. Without sentences, words are just ideas that do not make sense.

THE HUGE
CLOUD OF DUST
SWIRLED IN
AN ANGRY BLACK
FUNNEL

With a sentence, you can meet a new friend or teach a fact. You can even describe what a tornado looks like.

The huge cloud of dust swirled in an angry black funnel.

Sentences

WHICH KIND WOULD YOU LIKE?

Life is all about variety. Every day you eat different foods. You watch different TV shows. You spend time with different people. There is a lot of variety in your life. Sentences have variety, too.

WHAT'S THE SCOOP?

There are four basic kinds of sentences. Here's the best part: You usually don't have to think twice about which kind to use. Your purpose tells you whether you will use a statement, question, exclamation, or command.

These sentences make statements:

> Abraham Lincoln was the 16th president of the United States of America.
> The Tasmanian devil is my favorite animal.

You know a lot of facts. You have lots of ideas and opinions. When you write a sentence to give facts, ideas, or opinions, you are using a statement, or declarative sentence. Most sentences you write are statements. A statement ends with a period. Yes, that's a small dot. The dot, or period, shows the sentence is finished.

Any questions?

> Where did the cat hide?
> Can we swim in this pond?
> Why is the sky blue?

What would you do without questions? How would you find out about anything?

Questions, or interrogative sentences, are the second kind of sentence. Of course, a question ends with a question mark. A question mark does two things: It shows you that a sentence is a question, and it shows that the sentence has ended.

Exclamations are so exciting!

> That is the biggest dog I have ever seen!
> Anton forgot his backpack!

Do you want to show surprise, fear, excitement, or anger? Use an exclamation, or exclamatory sentence. An exclamation expresses strong feeling. It ends with an exclamation point. The exclamation point is like a surprised period. Exclamations can be fun. They can tell your readers that you are excited about your subject.

A Funny Kind of Sentence

Sentences want to have fun, too! Telling a joke is one way a sentence can have fun. The sentence that ends a joke and makes you laugh is called the punch line.

How do you keep a fish from smelling?

You hold its nose.

Take command.

> Always wear your seat belt.
> Stop!

Did you ever want to reign over your own little kingdom? Then you could command people to do whatever you wanted. In real life, you use commands all the time. They are imperative sentences. You use them to tell people to do something. They can end in periods or exclamation points.

CHECKUP ✔

Look at each group of words. Write "yes" if the group is a sentence that meets the four Fact Track requirements. Write "no" if it is not a sentence.

1. going around and around and around again.   _____

2. Raindrops glittered.   _____

3. Fred and Alissa and all their dogs and cats.   _____

4. On the hilltop, a coyote howled.   _____

5. In a forest with no lights.   _____

6. Trying to remember her name.   _____

7. Ten candles glowed atop the cake.   _____

8. No, I don't.   _____

9. too late for the parade?   _____

10. Swam in the pool.   _____

Fact Track
1. A sentence expresses a complete thought.
2. A sentence begins with a capital letter.
3. A sentence ends with end punctuation: a period, question mark, or exclamation point.
4. A sentence can make a statement, ask a question, express emotion, or tell someone what to do.

Answers are on page 21.

BRAIN GAMES

A Special Kind of Sentence

Have you ever heard of a *palindrome?* No, it's not a huge football stadium! It's a word or sentence that reads the same backward as forward. One famous sentence palindrome is "Madam, I'm Adam." Here's another sentence that's a palindrome:

Nurses run.

(Spell it backward. Separate the words. See?)

Here are some sentences. Figure out which letters go in the blanks to make them palindromes.

1. I d__d, d__d I?

2. Del__a s__il__d.

3. W__s it __ cat I __ __w?

4. D__t s__es T__d.

5. Ed i__ on __o s__de.

Answers are on page 21.

CHECKUP ✔

The sentences below do not have end punctuation. Decide whether each sentence is a statement, question, command, or exclamation. Write the sentence type. Then write the sentence with correct end punctuation.

1. Look at the monkeys playing

2. Is a platypus a bird or a mammal

3. Every octopus has eight long arms

4. When did the dinosaurs rule the earth

5. Wow, Spider-Man is great

Answers are on page 21.

BRAIN GAMES

Too Excited!

Have you ever received a note like the one below? If so, you might have told the writer to calm down. Revise Jenny's letter. Change most of her exclamations to statements, questions, or commands. Keep some exclamations. Choose them carefully.

Kerry!

I have to tell you what happened! Mr. Harvey liked my story! He's putting it in the school magazine! He said it's very original! He even liked the ending! Can you believe it?! Call me as soon as you get home! I'll tell you all about it! I'm so excited!

See you later!

Jenny

Answers are on page 21.

Too Many "!" Are Pointless

Go easy with exclamations. Too many can have the opposite effect of being exciting: They get boring. A reader cannot tell what is truly exciting because all the feelings seem the same. Some writers use two or more exclamation points at the end of a sentence. This is a no-no! Never use more than one end mark at the end of a sentence.

Subjects and Predicates

A Shopping List for a Sentence

Every sentence needs them. Most sentences are not greedy. They take one of each—sometimes two or three. But one of each is an absolute necessity. That's because it's necessary that the person listening or reading understands the subject or predicate even if it's not said or written.

> Bikers raced.
> Five mountain bikers raced down the steep hill.

Both of these are complete sentences. The first sentence has only two words. Yet it creates a full picture in your mind. Who or what is it about? Bikers. What did they do? raced. The second sentence gives more details.

Subject?

Bikers is the *subject* of the sentences. The subject is who or what the sentence is about. A complete sentence contains a subject. The subject may be a *noun*. A noun names a person, place, or thing. A subject can also be a *pronoun*. A pronoun is a word like they. It takes the place of a noun. In these sentences, the subject is a noun: Bikers.

Predicate?

A complete sentence also has a predicate. A *predicate* always has a verb. A verb names an action or a state of being. The predicate of a sentence tells what the subject does or is. In these sentences, the predicate is the verb raced. It tells us what the bikers are doing.

You can add other words to a sentence that describe the subject. The subject and all the words that describe it are called the *complete subject:*

> Five mountain bikers

You can add words that describe the predicate. The verb and all the words that describe it are called the *complete predicate:*

> raced down the steep hill.

PREDICATES WITH THE NON-ACTION VERB "TO BE"

The bread is fresh.
The best meal was breakfast.

Are these complete sentences? The bread does not perform any action, as the bikers did in the sentences above. But the first sentence has a verb, is. It is a form of the verb to be. The verb was, in the next sentence, is also a form of to be. Each of these verbs needs another word to be complete. An adjective may complete the verb, such as fresh in the first sentence. A noun can also complete the verb, such as breakfast in the second sentence. The verb to be with the adjective or noun that completes it and the other words that describe it form the complete predicate.

Forms of the Verb "To Be"

I am	I was	I have been
you are	you were	you have been
he, she, or it is	he, she, or it was	he, she, or it has been
we are	we were	we have been
they are	they were	they have been

QUESTIONS

Can James play?
Who says?

Are these questions complete sentences? The first one has a subject, *James.* It also has a verb, *can play.* The subject separates the two parts of the verb. Since the question has a subject and a verb, it is a complete sentence. But how about the second question? It has a verb, *says.* But what is the subject? The subject is *who*, a pronoun. (Find out more about pronouns in Chapter 4.) Because the question has a subject and a predicate, it is a complete sentence.

FUN FACT

Scientists wonder how language began. Some think the first sentences were one-word commands, like "Run!" The next kind were two-word statements, like "Fire hot." The next kind were questions, such as "Berry patches?"

BRAIN GAMES

In a conversation, you may not always use complete sentences. Read the dialogue below. Decide whether each group of words is a complete sentence or not.

1. Chris: What are you having for lunch?
2. Alex: Turkey sandwich.
3. How about you?
4. Chris: Crunchy peanut butter and grape jelly sandwich.
5. Alex: Don't you have that every day?
6. Chris: Only on Mondays, Wednesdays, Thursdays, and Fridays.
7. Alex: What about Tuesdays?
8. Chris: On Tuesdays I go a little crazy.
9. Alex: How?
10. Chris: I have creamy peanut butter and strawberry jam.

Sentence Checklist

Complete the sentence checklist. Consider each group of words by itself. The first example is done for you.

	Subject?	Predicate?	Complete Sentence?
The car swerved.	✓	✓	yes
1. A grizzly bear appeared.			
2. Jumped in front of the car.			
3. A huge animal with shaggy fur.			
4. Dad pressed the gas pedal.			
5. Got out of there fast!			
6. I wasn't a bit scared.			

Answers are on page 21.

Sentences and Sentence Fragments

Suppose a friend says these words to you: "Shouldn't let Moe eat socks." You want to know the whole story. *Who* shouldn't let Moe eat socks? *Who* is Moe? *What* did Moe do? *How* did he do it?

"Shouldn't let Moe eat socks" is a sentence fragment. A fragment is missing a subject or a predicate or sometimes both. A fragment leaves you wondering, who—what—how—*huh?*

If your friend wrote down the whole Moe story, it might look like this:

> Our dog Moe, a big Labrador. Got sick again. We took him to the vet. Who was a little upset. With us. Because Moe had been sick before. Giving us advice about Moe. Shouldn't let Moe eat socks.

This paragraph has many sentence fragments. They don't have all the necessary parts of a sentence.

Here's the paragraph with all the fragments corrected.

Our dog Moe, a big Lab, got sick again. We took him to the vet, who was a little upset with us. That is because Moe had had the same problem before. The vet gave us advice about Moe. The vet said that we shouldn't let him eat socks.

The next time you look for fragments in your writing, just remember your friend's dog Moe.

BRAIN GAMES

Complete Sentences—Complete Story

Some of the word groups below are complete sentences. They begin and end a story. The other word groups are sentence fragments. Put them in order to tell a logical story. Then correct the fragments.

Dad took my little brother Toby and me sledding.

Tipped over.

On a big hill with one tree.

Heading right for the tree.

Because he couldn't help Toby steer the sled.

Toby turned away from the tree.

Dad got upset.

At the last second.

Gave Toby a push downhill.

But he was okay!

Answers are on page 21.

Subjects

FIND THE SUBJECT

Let's see, I'm sure I put a subject in this sentence somewhere. Nope, that's not it. Aha!

You know that every sentence needs a subject. But in some sentences, the subject is not so easy to find. In a *declarative sentence*, the subject is usually at or near the beginning.

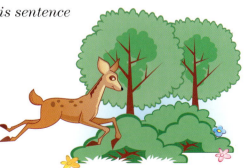

The deer darted into the woods.

Sometimes other words begin sentences.

> There are many surfers on the beach.

In the sentence above, the word *there* is at the beginning. In sentences that begin with *here* or *there*, the subject usually comes after the verb. In this sentence, the verb is *are*. What are? Surfers. Surfers is the subject of the sentence.

Are you looking for the subject of a *question?* All you need to do is change it to a declarative sentence, then find the verb, and ask *who* or *what?*

> Can penguins fly?
> Penguins can fly.
> Who can fly? Penguins.
> Penguins is the subject.

Many questions begin with the pronouns *who, what, when,* and *where.* Sometimes the pronoun is the subject.

> What happened?

Where is the subject in an *imperative sentence?*

> Kick the ball into the goal.

In an imperative sentence, or a command, the subject is you but it is not stated. It is implied:

> (You) Kick the ball into the goal.

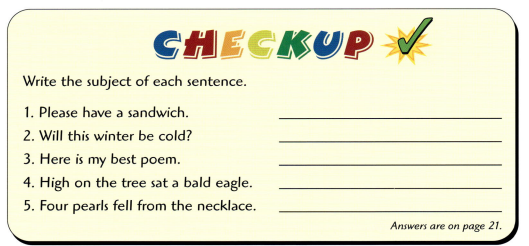

CHECKUP ✔

Write the subject of each sentence.

1. Please have a sandwich. _____

2. Will this winter be cold? _____

3. Here is my best poem. _____

4. High on the tree sat a bald eagle. _____

5. Four pearls fell from the necklace. _____

Answers are on page 21.

BRAIN GAMES

Sentence Secret/Secret Sentence

An important fact about sentence subjects is encoded in this message. The code is a number–alphabet code. 1 = A, 2 = B, 3 = C, and so on. Decode the message!

20 8 5   19 21 2 10 5 3 20   15 6   1   3 15 13 13 1 14 4   9 19   25 15 21.

_____ _____ _____ __ _____ _____ _____

Answers are on page 21.

Compound Sentences

BUILDING WITH SUBJECTS AND PREDICATES

Did you ever want to be an architect and design buildings? You could make the world's tallest building! You could make houses and offices with bricks, concrete, and steel.

In a similar way, you can build sentences. Subjects and predicates are the bricks and concrete of sentences. You can combine them in lots of ways. You could even build the world's longest sentence!

> The new recreation center is open. Many workers built it. Carpenters worked hard. Bricklayers worked hard. Families have a great new place for fun activities.

Each sentence in this paragraph has one subject and one verb. You can combine some of these sentences. You can make sentences with compound subjects. You can make sentences with compound predicates. You can also make compound sentences. *Compound* means putting two or more things together.

COMPOUND SUBJECTS

A compound subject is made up of two or more subjects joined by the conjunction and or or that share the same verb:

> Carpenters and bricklayers worked hard.

These subjects share the same predicate: *worked hard.* The sentence is a *simple sentence.*

COMPOUND PREDICATES

A compound predicate is made up of two or more predicates that share the same subject. These predicates have the same subject: *workers.*

> Workers poured the cement. Workers hammered nails.

You can combine them like this:

> Workers poured the cement and hammered nails.

Now you have a compound predicate.

COMPOUND SENTENCES

You can combine two sentences to make them into a compound sentence.

> The new recreation center is open, and families have a great new place for fun activities.

This sentence has two different subjects. The subjects are doing two different things. It is a *compound sentence.*

DOES A COMMA HAVE A PLACE?

Compound sentences need to be punctuated with commas because the two different subjects are doing two different things.

> The sidewalk was icy, and some people slipped.

Simple sentences do not need commas.

> People slipped and slid on the icy sidewalk.

Check whether you have a compound sentence, compound subject, or compound predicate before adding any commas.

CHECKUP ✓

Tell whether each sentence is a simple or a compound sentence.

1. Raccoons and skunks live in our neighborhood.

2. Once I even saw a coyote.

3. My dog Flash barks and growls at wild animals.

4. One night a raccoon got into the garage, and Flash went crazy.

5. I kept Flash in the house, and he was not happy about that.

Answers are on page 21.

Complex Sentences

MAKE SENTENCES WORK FOR YOU

Now that you know all about sentences, make them work for you. No lazy sentences around here! You can use what you know about compound sentences to build another kind of sentence—a complex sentence.

> Our team won, and the crowd cheered loudly.
> The crowd cheered loudly because our team won.

These two sentences say about the same thing. Yet the second sentence gives more information. It tells about the cause and effect between the main ideas of the sentence. It tells what happened and why it happened. The sentence has one main clause: The crowd cheered loudly. That's what happened. The second clause is because our team won. That's why it happened. The second clause is called a *dependent clause*—it depends on the main clause to make sense.

THE PARTS OF A COMPLEX SENTENCE

Here's what you find in a complex sentence:

> a main clause
> one or more dependent clauses

Dependent clauses can appear in different places in a sentence. They can serve different purposes in a sentence.

> Jimmy, who is invited to a sleepover, has a problem.

The dependent clause describes the subject of the sentence.

> Jimmy always has his retainer on when he goes to bed.
> He must decide whether he will take his retainer to the sleepover.

The dependent clauses describe the predicates of the sentences.

> What Jimmy wants is to leave his retainer at home.

The dependent clause is the subject of the sentence.

CHECKUP ✔

Tell whether each sentence is simple, compound, or complex.

1. Would you take a retainer to the sleepover if you were Jimmy?   _____

2. Will the new superhero movie come out in the fall, or will it be delayed until next year?   _____

3. Read an adventure book.   _____

4. You will find out what the characters do.   _____

5. You will enjoy reading the book.   _____

Answers are on page 21.

ANSWERS

page 8

CHECKUP

1) no; **2)** yes; **3)** no; **4)** yes; **5)** no;
6) no; **7)** yes; **8)** yes; **9)** no; **10)** no

page 9

A SPECIAL KIND OF SENTENCE

1) I did, did I?; **2)** Delia sailed.; **3)** Was it a cat I saw?; **4)** Dot sees Tod.; **5)** Ed is on no side.

CHECKUP

1) command — Look at the monkeys playing.

2) question — Is a platypus a bird or a mammal?

3) statement — Every octopus has eight long arms.

4) question — When did the dinosaurs rule the earth?

5) exclamation — Wow, Spider-Man is great!

page 10

TOO EXCITED!

Kerry,
I have to tell you what happened. Mr. Harvey liked my story! He's putting it in the school magazine. He said it's very original. He even liked the ending. Can you believe it? Call me as soon as you get home. I'll tell you all about it. I'm so excited!
See you later,
Jenny

page 13

CONVERSATION

1) complete sentence; **2)** not complete;
3) not complete; **4)** not complete;
5) complete; **6)** not complete;
7) not complete; **8)** complete
9) not complete; **10)** complete

SENTENCE CHECKLIST

	Subject?	Predicate?	Complete Sentence?
1.	✓	✓	yes
2.		✓	no
3.	✓		no
4.	✓	✓	yes
5.		✓	no
6.	✓	✓	yes

page 15

COMPLETE STORY

Dad took my little brother Toby and me sledding on a big hill with one tree. Dad gave Toby a push downhill. Soon Toby was heading right for the tree. Dad got upset because he couldn't help Toby steer the sled. Toby turned away from the tree at the last second. He tipped over. But he was okay!

page 16

CHECKUP

1) you; **2)** winter; **3)** poem; **4)** eagle;
5) pearls

page 17

SENTENCE SECRET/SECRET SENTENCE

The subject of a command is *you.*

page 19

CHECKUP

1) simple; **2)** simple; **3)** simple;
4) compound; **5)** compound

page 20

CHECKUP

1) complex; **2)** compound; **3)** simple;
4) complex; **5)** simple

Nouns
Name That Person, Place, or Thing!

Imagine a world without nouns. It's hard to do because nouns are anything that you can name. In a world without nouns, there would be a lot of pointing and picture drawing when you wanted to talk about a person, a feeling, a party, a game, or an animal.

Nouns are naming words. With them, you can name who, what, and where. You can name people, places, things, and ideas.

Here are some examples of nouns:

Person—sister, friend, Jon, Mrs. Johnson, Uncle Al
Place—bedroom, library, Main Street, Lake Erie, Miami, Africa
Thing—toy, computer, daisy, number
Ideas—happiness, beauty, freedom

BRAIN GAMES

Noun Puzzle

Answer the clues. Look at the number under each letter of your answers. Write the letters in the number grid on the opposite page. You can work back and forth until you complete the sentence in the grid. The answer is an important message about nouns.

A. The seed of wheat or rice

 $\overline{29}$ $\overline{14}$ $\overline{1}$ $\overline{27}$ $\overline{5}$

B. Put a liquid in a glass

 $\overline{12}$ $\overline{16}$ $\overline{4}$ $\overline{24}$

C. Not a woman, but a

 $\overline{8}$ $\overline{20}$ $\overline{17}$

D. Hat

 $\overline{21}$ $\overline{7}$ $\overline{18}$

E. Not win, but

 $\overline{19}$ $\overline{23}$ $\overline{10}$ $\overline{9}$

F. Tidy

 $\overline{28}$ $\overline{22}$ $\overline{11}$ $\overline{25}$

G. Female chickens

 $\overline{26}$ $\overline{13}$ $\overline{2}$ $\overline{15}$

H. The opposite of yes

 $\overline{6}$ $\overline{3}$

Naming the Subject

A noun is often the subject of a sentence. The subject of each sentence below is underlined. Each subject is a noun. Each noun is the name of something, or what something is called.

> Africa has many giant animals.
> The elephant is the largest land animal on Earth.
> A hippopotamus can weigh almost 3 tons.
> The rhinoceros is larger than the hippo.
> The giraffe can grow to about 18 feet high.

These sentences contain other nouns besides their subjects. *Animals, animal, Earth, tons, hippo,* and *high* are all nouns.

CHECKUP ✔

Underline each noun in the sentences below.

1. In what country are there more sheep than people?

2. Australia has about 10 sheep for every person.

3. Ranchers raise the sheep for food and wool.

4. Mary had a little lamb.

5. With only one lamb, Mary must not have been a shepherd in Australia.

Answers are on page 37.

1		2	3	4	5		6	7	8	9	10
11		12	13	14	15	16	17	,			
18	19	20	21	22	,		23	24			
25	26	27	28	29	.						

Answers are on page 37.

1 Noun + 1 Noun = 1 Compound Noun

What do the following words have in common?

sea horse   dragonfly   bullfrog

No, they are not weird creatures from a horror movie! Each word is a compound noun. This means it is made up of two smaller words. Some compound words, like *hot dog*, are written separately. Some, like *grown-up*, have a

Is this a sea horse? (No way!)

hyphen between the two parts. But most compound words are written as one word. There are lots of compound nouns. Sometimes you can figure out what they are by beginning with the meanings of the two words.

BRAIN GAMES

Compound Riddles

The answer to each of the following rhyming riddles is a compound noun. Figure out each one.

1. Despite its name, this stuff won't glue.
   If this paste did, you could not chew.   _____

2. You can't put it on bread with a spoon.
   This pretty bug comes out of a cocoon.   _____

3. Bushy ones are a good disguise.
   They're below the hair and above the eyes.   _____

Answers are on page 37.

Common Nouns

JUST PART OF THE CROWD

The Singer children, Aaron and Josh, were in a choir. One day they heard the director say, "I want all Singers to sing very loudly on this song." Aaron and Josh were amazed but ready to belt out the tune. When the song began, the brothers were surprised to hear all the other children singing loudly, too. Then they knew they had not understood the director. He had meant "singers," not "Singers."

What is one difference between Singers singing loudly by themselves or as part of a group? One difference is between a proper noun and a common noun. Regarding the brothers, "Singers" is a proper noun. It names a family name. The word "singers" as the choir director meant it is a common noun. It does not refer to the brothers but to all children in the choir.

> The girls visited the museum this weekend.
> The statue stands on an island in the bay.

How are all the highlighted words alike? First, all of them are nouns. Second, they are *common nouns*. Each noun names a general person, place, or thing, not one particular thing. Common nouns are not capitalized.

Proper Nouns

SPECIFIC AND SPECIAL

Proper nouns name particular persons, places, or things. They help you tell one person, month of the year, or day of the week from another.

You are a special person. You wouldn't like it if people got you confused with your friend down the street. The month of May is special, too—not to be confused with December, and it would be hard to mistake a Monday morning for a Saturday morning.

> Sara and Emily visited the Field Museum on Saturday.
> The Statue of Liberty stands on Liberty Island in Upper New York Bay.

How are all these highlighted words alike? They are proper nouns instead of common nouns. Who goes to the museum? Not just any girls, but specific girls: Sara and Emily. The Field Museum is a particular museum. Saturday is a particular weekend day. What statue stands on the island? Not just any statue, but the Statue of Liberty. Liberty Island is a particular island. Proper nouns are capitalized.

Proper Nouns Name People
Cristina Perez
Sean Jones
Benjamin Franklin
Sally Ride

Proper Nouns Name Places	Proper Nouns Name Things
Seattle, Washington	Metropolitan Museum of Art
Lake Michigan	World War II
Rocky Mountains	McKinley School
South America	Girl Scouts of America

CHECKUP ✔

Each boldface word below is a noun. Decide whether each one is a common noun or a proper noun. On a sheet of paper, draw two columns and title each one "Common Nouns" and "Proper Nouns." Write the words in the correct columns.

1. Is **Mount Etna** an angry **mountain**?

2. This **volcano** in **Sicily** often blows its **top.**

3. Visit the **Hawaii Volcanoes National Park** on the **island** of **Hawaii.**

4. There **tourists** can watch **lava** pouring from **Kilauea.**

Answers are on page 37.

More Categories for Common Nouns

A common noun is either concrete or abstract. Also, a common noun may be a collective noun.

CONCRETE AND ABSTRACT

What do you know about concrete? You can touch it for one thing. It feels hard and cold and rough. Some nouns are described as "concrete." *Concrete nouns* name things that you can recognize with your senses. You can see, hear, touch, taste, or smell them.

Here are some examples of concrete nouns:

elephant	piano
rock	apple
perfume	

Other nouns name ideas or feelings. They are *abstract nouns.* You cannot see, hear, touch, taste, or smell abstract nouns. You recognize them with your mind.

Here are some examples of abstract nouns:

peace   selfishness
beauty   freedom
fear

COLLECTIVE NOUNS—GROUP RATES

Some common nouns name a group of people, places, or things. They are *collective nouns.*

Here are some examples of collective nouns:

family   herd
class   team

A collective noun may be singular or plural in a sentence. It depends on whether the sentence is about the group as a whole or the individuals in the group.

The *class goes* on a field trip. (The class goes as a group.)
The *family go* their own ways on the weekend. (The family members go as individuals.)

BRAIN GAMES

Animals in Groups

Some collective nouns name groups of specific kinds of animals. You've heard of a *flock of sheep* and a *herd of cows. Flock* and *herd* are collective nouns. See if you can match each animal to its collective noun. Draw a line to show the name of each animal's group. (*Hint:* One of the words describes a characteristic of one of the animals.)

lion	band
gorilla	gaggle
ant	pride
kangaroo	pod
goose	troop
whale	pack
wolf	colony

Why did the father lion boast when he showed his family pictures?

He had great pride!

Answers are on page 37.

CHECKUP ✔

Find the proper nouns that should be capitalized but are not. Find the common nouns that should not be capitalized but are. Correct each one.

1. My favorite Season is Summer, but December is my favorite Month.
2. We studied the revolutionary war in History.
3. The sign pointed South, but we knew san francisco was due west.
4. Which Holiday is on the fourth thursday of November?
5. One famous Artist from New york was grandma Moses.

Answers are on page 37.

BRAIN GAMES

Knock-Knock Jokes

Knock-knock jokes often use proper nouns. Complete each joke below with one of the following names: Wendy, Amos, Tarzan, Arthur

1. Knock knock. Who's there? ____. ____ who? ____ stripes forever!

2. Knock knock. Who's there? ____. ____ who? ____ quito bit me!

3. Knock knock. Who's there? ____. ____ who? ____ any dogs in your house?

4. Knock knock. Who's there? ____. ____ who? ____ you get home from school?

Answers are on page 37.

Singular and Plural Nouns

ONE OR MORE

Choices, choices! The video store has hundreds of movies, and you get to choose one movie. The library has thousands of books, but you choose one book. *Movie* and *book* are singular nouns. Each refers to one thing.

A bird built a nest in the garage.
The doctor checked Jody's ears.
The city is crowded on Friday afternoon.

Bird, doctor, city. Each of these is a *singular noun* because it names one person, place, or thing. The sentences are about one bird, one doctor, and one city. Of course, you can also talk about more than one bird, one doctor, and one city.

The birds chirp happily as the sun rises.
Doctors rushed down the halls of the hospital.
Many American cities have buses, trains, and subways.

You can change the form of a singular noun. You can make it a plural noun. Then you can tell about more than one person, place, or thing.

You often add *-s* or *-es* to a singular noun to make a plural noun:

tiger	tigers
lunch	lunches

But you form some plurals in different ways:

woman	women

The words *a*, *an*, and *the* are often used before a singular noun. The word *the* can also be used before a plural noun.

WE WANT MORE!

Mom: What did you and
Grandpa have for lunch?
Megan: Sandwiches and
strawberries.

Plural means more than one. Without plural nouns, Megan could not have answered that question. One is often just not enough! So you need to know how to form the plurals of nouns.

Chapter Two

Our team scored one goal. The other team scored three goals.
In the first sentence, the noun *goal* is singular. In the second sentence, the noun *goals* is plural.

Here's a list of some singular nouns followed by their plurals.

chair	chairs	child	children
baby	babies	bench	benches
shelf	shelves		

You know you can make many nouns plural by adding an -s at the end. But you can't count on this for all nouns. Look again at the nouns list. Except for the first noun *chair*, all the nouns have more changes than adding just -s. If you learn a few rules, you can form the plural of any noun.

1. For many nouns, just add -s to the singular noun to form the plural.

car	cars	friend	friends
sock	socks	boy	boys
teacher	teachers	turkey	turkeys

2. Some nouns end with a consonant followed by *y*. Form the plural by changing the *y* to *ie*. Then add -s.

family	families	penny	pennies
cherry	cherries		

3. Some singular nouns end in *s*, *ch*, *sh*, or *x*. To form the plural of these nouns, add -es.

class	classes	box	boxes
branch	branches	Jones	Joneses
wish	wishes		

4. Some singular nouns end in *f* or *fe*. *Most of the time,* you change them to *ve* and then add -s.

leaf	leaves	thief	thieves
knife	knives		

5. Some nouns end with a vowel followed by *o*. You form the plural of *most* of these by adding -s.

zoo	zoos	radio	radios

6. Some nouns end with a consonant followed by *o*. You form the plural of most of these by adding *-es*.

      zero   zeroes   potato   potatoes

7. Some nouns have irregular plurals. This means you do not add *-s* or *-es*. Instead, the word changes in a different way.

      child   children
      man   men
      mouse   mice

CHECKUP

Write the plural of each boldface noun shown in the sentences.

1. Put the **tomato** in the **sandwich.**
2. The **wolf** howled.
3. The **woman** walked along the **beach.**
4. Did you enjoy the **video** of the **rodeo?**
5. The **goose** made a **fuss.**

Answers are on page 37.

BRAIN GAMES

Camp Memories

Jeff's letter contains some errors in the plural forms of nouns. Write each incorrect plural noun correctly.

Dear Jeff,

Camp is great! There are flys everywhere. It has rained for three days. We're not allowed to listen to radioes. The beachs have lots of rocks. You have to be careful walking on the paths. Snakes hide under the leafs. There are no horses. But we can ride donkies. Anyway, I guess you can see what a good time I'm having!

Your friend,
Tom

Answers are on page 37.

Slipups

Some people add "apostrophe s" to make proper nouns plural:

The Menoni's and the Weiss's came to dinner.

This is wrong. Remember, apostrophes show possession. The correct way to make these proper nouns plural is to add -s or -es.

The Menonis and the Weisses came to dinner.

Possessive Nouns Show Ownership

Did you ever write *Jackies jacket* when you meant *Jackie's jacket?* Or *I like skunk's* when you meant *I like skunks?* This section will teach you all you need to know about using "apostrophe s" correctly.

PESTY PUNCTUATION?

Salina's painting is excellent. Her pictures' colors impress her art teacher. The other students' work is good, too. But my sister's talent stands out.

Apostrophes seem to hover over the paragraph above like hungry mosquitoes. What's up with all the apostrophes in the paragraph? In each case, an apostrophe shows the possession of one noun by another noun. Look at the phrase "Salina's painting." The noun *painting* is the subject of the sentence. The word *Salina's* tells more about the painting. The *'s* shows Salina's "possession" of the painting. In other words, Salina is the creator of the painting. The next sentence contains an apostrophe, too. But this time the word ends with *s'*. This means that the word *pictures* is plural.

The rules for making nouns possessive are easier than you think. But first you have to know when to make a noun possessive.

MAKE SURE A POSSESSIVE IS REALLY POSSESSIVE

Should you use an apostrophe to show possession?

Look at the phrase (a group of two or more words) that you think may need an apostrophe. Make sure the phrase contains two nouns. Then make sure one noun "possesses" the other.

In each phrase given below, look at the first word and consider it without the *'s*. Are *dog*, *Carly*, and *the Murphys* nouns? Yes. Are *tail*, *poem*, and *yard* nouns? Yes. Read each phrase. You can see that the tail belongs to the dog, the poem belongs to Carly, and the yard belongs to the Murphys. So each is a possessive phrase. An apostrophe is used correctly in each phrase to show possession.

> dog's tail   Carly's poem   the Murphys' yard

HOW TO FORM POSSESSIVES

Once you are sure you have written a possessive phrase, you need to use an apostrophe to show that the first noun is possessive.

1. To make a singular noun possessive, add *'s*.

the scooter of Stacy	Stacy's scooter
the nest of the bird	bird's nest
the design of the dress	dress's design
the homework of Marcus	Marcus's homework

Notice the nouns *dress* and *Marcus*. They are singular nouns that end with *s*. Because they are singular, you add *'s* to make them possessive.

2. To make a plural noun ending in *s* possessive, add an apostrophe <u>after</u> the *s*.

the food for the puppies	the puppies' food
the trip of the Smiths	the Smiths' trip

3. To make a plural noun that does *not* end in *s* possessive, add *'s*.

the toys of the children	the children's toys
the wings of the geese	the geese's wings

Use two steps to make a noun possessive. First, make sure you have spelled the singular or plural form of the noun correctly. Then add *'s* or just an apostrophe correctly to show possession.

CHECKUP ✔

Write a possessive phrase to replace each phrase in parentheses.

1. Marie made all the (costumes of the actors).
2. Ken cleans the (cages of the animals) every day.
3. The (plan of the pitcher) was to strike out three batters.
4. Everyone sang along with the (music of the piano player).
5. The (authors of the books) read their stories.

Answers are on page 37.

BRAIN GAMES

Possessive Hink Pinks

A hink pink is a riddle whose answer is two rhyming words that are synonyms for words in the riddle. The answer words are usually an adjective and a noun. Each rhyming word has one syllable.

In these hink pinks, the first word is possessive. Be sure to write each possessive correctly. Example: stares from the chef <u>cook's</u> <u>looks</u>

1. the conversations between 2 kittens   _____ _____
2. homes for lady chickens   _____ _____
3. a young lady's white necklace   _____ _____
4. carpets for insects   _____ _____
5. royal woman's denim pants   _____ _____

Answers are on page 37.

Gerunds

AN ACTIVE KIND OF NOUN

Lots of words for activities end in *-ing*. They look like verbs, but they're nouns! They're called *gerunds*.

> Bicycling is fun. So are swimming, skating, skiing, stamp collecting, knitting, painting, and hiking.

In this next sentence, an *-ing* word, *skating*, is part of the verb. It describes the action of the sentence's subject.

> Sarah is skating.

In the next sentence, *skating* is the subject of the sentence. The word *skating* is not a verb here—it is a noun.

> Skating is Sarah's favorite thing in the whole world.

A gerund is an *-ing* word that serves as a noun in a sentence. The following sentences contain gerunds.

> Bicycling keeps Jack in shape.
> Terri's hobby is hiking.
> Beth started knitting last year.

Gerunds can serve different roles in sentences. Sometimes they are the subject, as in these sentences.

> Smiling will brighten your mood.
> Driving to Florida was Dad's plan.
> Reading takes Jeremy on many adventures.

In the following sentences, gerunds are not the subject. They serve different roles. Still, each gerund serves as a noun in the sentence.

> James likes singing in the shower.
> Katie spends lots of time on her sculpting.
> The hardest part of soccer is running.

CHECKUP ✔

The sentences below contain several *-ing* words. In two cases, the *-ing* word is a verb. All the others are gerunds that serve as nouns. Write each *-ing* word. Tell whether it is a verb or a gerund.

1. Skiing in the Olympics is Tim's goal.
2. Amy is bringing her little sister to the party.
3. Can you read Matt's handwriting?
4. Michelle's hobby, rock climbing, can be dangerous.
5. Jay was trying out a new tennis racket.

Answers are on page 37.

Using Nouns

COULD YOU BE MORE SPECIFIC?

> The place was dark and shadowy. A man hid behind some things. Some creatures began to surround him. Soon a scary noise broke the silence.

Suppose a friend gave the summary above to tell you about a movie. Yawn. You probably would not rush out to see that film. But what if your friend gave this description?

> The laboratory was dark and shadowy. A scientist hid behind the microscopes and Bunsen burners. Some space aliens began to surround him. Soon a scary whine broke the silence.

What a difference specific nouns can make! The first summary contains vague nouns like *place* and *things*. The second summary contains specific nouns like *laboratory* and *microscopes*. The first paragraph is not every exciting. The second one is specific and concrete. You can form mental pictures of the details in the movie.

When you write, use specific nouns. Sometimes you can use a proper noun in place of a common noun. Sometimes you can use a concrete noun in place of an abstract noun. A *synonym* is a word with the same or similar meaning as a particular word. You can use a thesaurus to find interesting synonyms for the nouns you use. A thesaurus is like a dictionary, but it contains only synonyms (having the same meaning) and antonyms (opposites) of words.

Q: Did you hear about the *crash* of the thesaurus delivery truck?

A: Yes! Witnesses said it was a disaster, a calamity, a collision, a wreck, a misadventure, a catastrophe, a smashup, and a mishap.

Answers

pages 22–23

NOUN PUZZLE

A) grain; B) pour; C) man; D) cap;
E) lose; F) neat; G) hens; H) no
Sentence: A noun names a person, place, or thing.

CHECKUP

1) In what <u>country</u> are there more <u>sheep</u> than <u>people?</u> 2) <u>Australia</u> has about 10 <u>sheep</u> for every <u>person.</u> 3) <u>Ranchers</u> raise the <u>sheep</u> for <u>food</u> and <u>wool.</u> 4) <u>Mary</u> had a little <u>lamb.</u> 5) With only one <u>lamb,</u> <u>Mary</u> must not have been a <u>shepherd</u> in <u>Australia.</u>

page 24

COMPOUND RIDDLES

1) toothpaste; 2) butterfly; 3) eyebrows

page 26

CHECKUP

Common Nouns: mountain; volcano; top; island; tourists; lava.
Proper Nouns: Mount Etna; Sicily; Hawaii Volcanoes National Park; Hawaii; Kilauea

page 27

ANIMALS IN GROUPS

lion—pride; gorilla—band; ant—colony; kangaroo—troop; goose—gaggle; whale—pod; wolf—pack

page 28

CHECKUP

1. My favorite season is summer, but December is my favorite month.
2. We studied the Revolutionary War in history.
3. The sign pointed south, but we knew San Francisco was due west.
4. Which holiday is on the fourth Thursday of November?

5. One famous artist from New York was Grandma Moses.

KNOCK-KNOCK JOKES

1) Tarzan; 2) Amos; 3) Arthur; 4) Wendy

page 31

CHECKUP

1) tomatoes, sandwiches; 2) wolves 3) women, beaches; 4) videos, rodeos 5) geese, fusses

CAMP MEMORIES

Dear Jeff,
Camp is great! There are *flies* everywhere. It has rained for three days. We're not allowed to listen to *radios.* The *beaches* have lots of rocks. You have to be careful walking on the paths. Snakes hide under the *leaves.* There are no horses. But we can ride *donkeys.* Anyway, I guess you can see what a good time I'm having!
Your friend,
Tom

page 34

CHECKUP

1. Marie made all the actors' costumes.
2. Ken cleans the animals' cages every day.
3. The pitcher's plan was to strike out three batters.
4. Everyone sang along with the piano player's music.
5. The books' authors read their stories.

POSSESSIVE HINK PINKS

1) cats' chats; 2) hens' pens; 3) girl's pearls; 4) bugs' rugs; 5) queen's jeans

page 35

CHECKUP

1) Skiing—gerund; 2) bringing—verb 3) handwriting—gerund; 4) climbing—gerund; 5) trying—verb

Verbs
Get into the Act

How do you tell people what you did or how you felt? You use verbs: *I jumped about a mile in the air. I was so scared!* Verbs are the heart of a sentence. They show actions and feelings.

Action Verbs

VARIETIES IN THE GARDEN

The garden of *action verbs* grows two types: physical action and mental action. These sentences use action verbs that tell about a physical action or actions that can be seen:

I jump. They run.

Not all action verbs tell about physical action. Some action verbs tell about mental or other unseen actions:

He thinks. She knows.

BRAIN GAMES

Physical or Mental Action?

Action verbs can show physical action, like *run* and *jump.* They can also show mental action, like *wonder* and *enjoy.* Think of an action verb for each sentence. Tell whether it is physical or mental.

I _____ at the dog, "Stop!" _____

Then I _____ after the dog. _____

The dog _____ its tail. _____

It _____ that this was a fine game! _____

I just _____ my hat back. _____

Answers are on page 57.

Linking Verbs and Company

Not all verbs show action. *Linking verbs,* also called *state-of-being verbs,* show a condition or a state of being:

> I am happy. The pizza tastes good.

Some verbs just tell how things are.

> How was the party? It was great fun.

Have you ever noticed what these verbs do? They don't call attention to themselves. They call attention to a word that comes after them.

Linking verbs link the subject with a word that describes or identifies it. Most linking verbs are made from some form of the verb *be.* These include *am, is, are, were, be, being, been.*

> I am a good reader. This book is exciting!

SUBJECT, MEET PREDICATE

Remember, they call them linking verbs for a reason. The part of a sentence with the verb is called the predicate. Linking verbs link a word in the predicate back to the subject. The word may identify the subject or describe it. Think of the three sentence parts as links in a chain.

> A whale is a mammal.—The predicate word identifies the subject.

> A whale is enormous!—The predicate word describes the subject.

VERBS OF THE SENSES

Verbs that tell about the five senses can also be linking verbs. The words *appear, become, feel, look, remain, seem, smell, sound, stay,* and *taste* can be linking verbs.

> The cookies smell great! The water tastes salty.

Tricks

How to tell when verbs of the senses are linking verbs.

The water *tastes* salty. Ellen *tasted* the cookies.

How can you tell when they are linking verbs? Take out the sense verb and put in a form of the verb *be*. If the sentence still makes sense, the verb is a linking verb.

The water *tastes* salty. The water *is* salty.
Tastes is a linking verb.

Ellen *tasted* the cookies. Ellen *is* the cookies.
Tasted is not a linking verb. It is an action verb.

CHECKUP

Identify or Describe?

Add a predicate word to finish each sentence. Does your word describe the subject or identify it? Circle "Identify" or "Describe."

1. A cookie tastes _____. Identify   Describe

2. A cracker tastes _____. Identify   Describe

3. My mother is a _____. Identify   Describe

4. My grandpa was a _____. Identify   Describe

5. A caterpillar becomes a _____. Identify   Describe

6. A butterfly looks _____. Identify   Describe

Answers are on page 57.

BRAIN GAMES

Making Connections

Add a linking verb to finish each sentence. Pick verbs from the Word Bank.

1. Hello. I _____ Lee.

2. Who _____ you?

3. This _____ my dog Oscar.

4. Your dog _____ cool.

5. He _____ friendly.

6. His bark _____ like a car starting.

7. His fur _____ like wire.

Word Bank

am

is

feels

are

looks

sounds

seems

Answers are on page 57.

Direct Objects—Who Did What to Whom?

A sentence can be as simple as one subject and one action verb. Someone or something acts:

> Maria worked.

Most sentences tell more than this. After the verb, there is someone or something that receives the action:

> Maria planted flowers.

In this sentence, *flowers* is a direct object. A *direct object* follows an action verb. It answers the question "What?" or "Whom?" about the verb. As you can tell, only an action verb can have a direct object.

BRAIN GAMES

Director of Direct Objects

Finish the story. Make up a direct object for each blank.

Rick and Mary are friends. Rick asked

_____ to come to his house.

Mary brought her _____.

They played _____ for hours. Then they ate _____.

Answers are on page 57.

Indirect Objects

A sentence with a direct object sometimes has an *indirect object*. It comes before the direct object and answers the question "To what?" or "To whom?"

subject	verb	direct object
Ms. Jones	told	a story.

Told what? *Story* is the direct object.

subject	verb	indirect object	direct object
Ms. Jones	told	the children	a story.

Told what? *Story* is the direct object. Told a story to whom? *Children* is the indirect object.

A direct object comes after an action verb. An indirect object comes *before* the direct object—it cannot be the caboose on the sentence train:

Mom sang me a song.

CHECKUP ✔

Using Verbs, Objects, and Predicate Words

Find the underlined verbs. Give each action verb a star. Give each linking verb a check. Finish the story with words from the Word Bank.

Jim <u>found</u> a strange _____. It <u>looked</u> very ___. He said, "Maybe it <u>is</u> a ___."

But it <u>had</u> _____. Its shell <u>felt</u> _____. Then he <u>gave</u> ___ a poke. The thing

<u>rolled</u> _____ into a ball." I <u>will call</u> _____ Roly-Poly," said Jim.

Word Bank

Words Used as

Direct Objects: animal, legs, you   **Indirect Objects:** it, itself, hard

Predicate Words: odd, worm

Answers are on page 57.

Main Verbs and Helping Verbs

What are you doing right now? Well, duh! *You are reading this paragraph!* Now find the verb in the preceding sentence. Do you see that the verb has two words in it? *(are reading)* You have discovered another fact about verbs. They can be made up of two or more words.

A LITTLE HELP, PLEASE!

What is the verb in this sentence?

Jerod takes photographs of animals.

The verb is the word *takes*. Some sentences need verbs with more than one word.

Jerod is taking photographs of chimpanzees.
They are watching him curiously.

Verbs like this have two parts: a helping verb and a main verb.

Helping Verb	Main Verb
is	taking
are	watching

You can think of helping verbs as assistants. They help the main verb express action or a condition.

Here is a list of 23 words that can be used as helping verbs. Notice they are listed in six "families." All the families have three members, except the *be* family—it has eight members.

23 Helping Verbs

may	be	do	should	have	will
might	being	does	could	had	can
must	been	did	would	has	shall
	am	(main)		(main)	
	are				
	is				
	was				
	were				
	(main)				

Some verbs in this chart can also be used alone as the main verb. Verbs in the *be*, *do*, and *have* families can be helping verbs or main verbs (main).

For example, in the *be* family:

> Angela is learning the helping verbs.—Helping verb: is; main verb: learning
> She is in my class at school.—Main verb: is

Tricks

Help with Helping Verbs

To help you learn the 23 helping verbs, here is a story with a moral. The moral gives you the top word of the six families of helping verbs.

Mr. Do was rich. His relatives wondered who would inherit Mr. Do's fortune. When he died, the relatives searched for a will. Alas! They didn't find one. They did not get one penny of Mr. Do's money.

Moral: It *may be* that Mr. *Do should have a will.*

HOW MANY HELPERS DOES A MAIN VERB NEED?

A sentence can contain up to three helping verbs with the main verb.

> The dog was chasing the cat.—One helping verb: was
> The dog has been chasing the cat.—Two helping verbs: has been
> The dog must have been chasing the cat.—Three helping verbs: must have been

Helping verbs usually sit next to the main verb, but they can be separated. Other words can come between them. This is okay. They are still on the same team!

> Do you see the panda?—
> Verb = do see
> It is always sleeping.—
> Verb = is sleeping

FUN FACT

When you see an *-ing* verb, such as *smiling*, watch for a helping verb. Main verbs with *-ing* need a helping verb to make sense.

> Pat smiling about the joke.—verb not complete
> Pat is smiling about the joke.—verb complete

BRAIN GAMES

Story Completion

Use verbs in the blanks to finish the story. Pick at least one helping verb and one main verb from the Word Bank for each answer. *Hint:* One of the helping verbs is used more than once.

Word Bank			
Helping Verbs		**Main Verbs**	
was	must	thought	sleeping
do	have	swinging	sprung
had		get	attached

Once upon a time, Tiger _____ _____ in a tree. Monkey _____ _____ through the forest. He _____ _____ _____ the tiger tail was a vine. Before Monkey knew it, that vine _____ _____ to life! It _____ _____ to one mad tiger.

Moral: If you swing in the forest, _____ not _____ a tiger by the tail!

Answers are on page 57.

Present, Past, and Future Tenses

See, saw, will see. These are all forms of the verb *see.* How do you know which form to use when? Don't let verbs gang up on you! To use verbs correctly, you have to know what time it is.

QUICK-CHANGE ARTISTS

Verbs are quick-change artists. They have different forms, called tenses. The tense changes to show time. Remember that verbs show action or state of being. Did the action or state of being happen in the past, in the present, or in the future? Verb tense tells you.

Present Tense	Ed is a firefighter.	He fights fires.
Past Tense	He was at work.	He drove the fire truck.
Future Tense	He will be home later.	He will sleep well tonight.

The *present tense* tells about an action or a condition that is constant or tells a general truth:

Gold costs a lot.
Bears sleep in the winter.

It also tells about an action or a condition that exists only for now:

I am hungry.

Present Tense Forms

Notice that some present tense verbs end in –s or –es. When the subject is singular (naming one person, place, or thing), add –s or –es to the base form.

Mia *loves* tools. She *repairs* things around the house.

If the subject is plural (naming two or more), use the base form of the verb.

The squirrels *love* birdseed. They *raid* the bird feeder every day.

For more about when to add –s and –es, see Making Subjects and Verbs Agree on page 55.

The *past tense* tells about an action or a condition that was started and finished in the past. Most verbs change to the past tense when you add *-ed* or *-d* to the base form. Other verbs change their spelling when they change to past tense.

> She visited me last week. (visit—visited)
> We saw that movie then. (see—saw)

The *future tense* tells about an action or a condition that will take place in the future. Here you use the base form of the verb with *will* or *shall*.

> The bus will pick you up at 7:00. (pick—will pick)
> We shall win the game. (win—shall win)

To help you know which verb tense is correct, use the checking trick of "Today, Yesterday, and Tomorrow": Today he jumps. Yesterday he jumped. Tomorrow he will jump.

All Mixed Up

In this letter, cross out each mixed-up verb (shown underlined). Write the correct verb tense that fits the time when the action or condition occurs.

Dear Grandma and Grandpa,

How <u>were</u> you? I <u>will hope</u> you feel fine. Right now, I <u>was</u> very wet. That is because Daddy and I just <u>washing</u> the dog. It <u>will be</u> quite a show.

Pluto <u>will shake</u> as though he was freezing. In fact, the water <u>is</u> warm. When we put on the shampoo, he <u>hang</u> his head. He seemed to be saying, "Why <u>were</u> you punishing me?" Then we <u>rinsing</u> him off. He was so happy to be out of the tub, he <u>will wag</u> his whole body while we <u>dry</u> him.

Answers are on page 57.

Perfect Tenses

I see. I saw. I seen. Wait a minute! That last part doesn't sound right. When should you use that third form of the verb? You are about to find out when it is PERFECT-ly sensible!

WHAT'S PERFECT ABOUT THEM?

You have learned about simple past, present, and future tenses. Do you understand them? Good! Now hear this: There are more verb tenses! The *perfect tense* verbs use *has*, *have*, or *had* with a past form of the main verb. This past verb form, called the *past participle*, is the form used with a helping verb. (*Note:* The past and past participle forms of verbs are discussed later in the chapter on page 52.)

> She has seen the movie.
> I have seen it, too.
> They had seen it before we did.

Present perfect tense tells about an action or a condition that happened at some time in the past. The exact time is not important. Present perfect tense cannot be used with exact time words such as "yesterday" or "last week."

> Josh has finished his project.—Present perfect tense is correct.
> Josh finished his project yesterday.—Simple past tense is correct.

Past perfect tense tells about a past action or condition that began and ended before some other past event. To form this tense, use *had* plus the past participle.

> Joe had read the book before he saw the movie.

Future perfect tense tells about a future action or condition that will begin and end before another future event. Form this tense by using *will have* or *shall have* plus a past participle.

> By summertime, I will have learned to swim.

BRAIN GAMES

Timing Is Everything

On a separate piece of paper, rewrite each sentence below. Change the verb from past tense to present perfect tense. Add words to give the idea that the action began at some indefinite time in the past.

Example: My aunt gave me a toy for my birthday.
           My aunt has given me toys for my birthday for years.

1. The cherry trees were in bloom.

2. I wrote stories and poems.

3. The team played well.

Answers are on page 57.

Things that Make You Go, "Huh?"

Q. Why do they call it *present* perfect tense if it tells about a past action?

A. It does actually express past time. *Present* refers to the tense of the helping verbs *has* or *have.*

Examples:

Tom has ridden his bicycle.

He has washed the dog.

The girls have sung in the choir.

Progressive Forms

Whew! Six tenses so far. Is that all? Not yet! There is another set of six tenses! They are all about continuing action. Shall we continue?

WHERE *BE* MEETS *-ING*

So far, you have learned about six verb tenses: present, past, future, present perfect, past perfect, and future perfect. Each of these tenses also has a progressive form to express continuing action. To make the *progressive tenses*, use a *be* verb with the *-ing* form of a verb.

Present
They *jump*.

Present Progressive
They *are jumping*.

Past
They *jumped*.

Past Progressive
They *were jumping*.

Future
They *will jump*.

Future Progressive
They *will be jumping*.

Present Perfect
They *have jumped*.

Present Perfect Progressive
They *have been jumping*.

Past Perfect
They *had jumped*.

Past Perfect Progressive
They *had been jumping*.

Future Perfect
They *will have jumped*.

Future Perfect Progressive
They *will have been jumping*.

Let's look at two of the progressive tenses: present progressive and past progressive. How do you tell about an action that is going on as you speak or as you write? Use the present progressive tense.

> She is talking to Hank on the phone. — ongoing action
> She talks to him every afternoon. — repeated or usual action (present tense)

Do you see how present progressive tense is different from the simple present tense?

How do you think the past progressive tense is formed? That's right. Use a past form of *be* (*was* or *were*) with the *-ing* verb.

> She was talking to Hank when I got home. — Action was going on in the past when some other action occurred.

BRAIN GAMES

How Progressive Are You?

Finish each sentence. Write the form of the verb (shown in parentheses) to fit the situation.

1. The cat _____ a bath now. (be + take; present progressive tense)

2. Her kittens _____ all over her. (be + climb; present progressive tense)

3. This morning, mama cat _____ her kittens to hunt. (be + teach; past progressive tense)

4. The whole gang _____ in the backyard. (has + be + play; past perfect progressive tense)

5. Kittens at play _____ skills for life. (be + learn; present progressive tense)

6. Next, mama cat _____ her kittens to give themselves a bath! (be + teach; future progressive tense)

Answers are on page 57.

Irregular Verbs

Mother: What's wrong?
Little Girl: The bench I sitted on gived me a splinter.

Can you see how a young child would think these verbs are right? As you have learned, not all verbs fit the regular pattern for forming tenses.

VERB PARTS

Every verb has three parts: present, past, and past participle. These parts are used to make all the tenses. For regular verbs, the past is formed by adding *-ed* to the present. The past participle is the same as the past. It is used with the verbs *have, has,* and *had* to form the perfect tenses. Look at these verb parts.

Present	Past	Past Participle
talk	talked	(have) talked
cry	cried	(have) cried
hug	hugged	(have) hugged

Do you see that some regular verbs change their spelling a little to make the past verb part? If the present form ends in *y*, the *y* changes to *i* when you add *-ed*. If the regular verb has a short vowel sound and a single final consonant, the final consonant doubles when you add *-ed*.

RULE BREAKERS

For every rule, there are exceptions. You guessed it. Not all verbs follow the *-ed* rule. A number of verbs form the past part in irregular ways. *Irregular verbs* are verbs whose past forms are spelled differently than their present forms. Some irregular verbs also have a past participle that is different from the past form.

	Present	Past	Past Participle
REGULAR	play	played	(have) played
IRREGULAR	hear	heard	(have) heard—same as past
IRREGULAR	write	wrote	(have) written—different from past

GRIN AND MEMORIZE THEM!

There is no one rule for learning irregular verb forms. The best advice is to memorize them or become so familiar with the irregular forms that using them is automatic and sounds right to you. A list of some common irregular verbs is on the next page.

Parts of Irregular Verbs

Present	Past	Past Participle
am/is/are	was/were	(have) been
begin	began	(have) begun
come	came	(have) come
do	did	(have) done
draw	drew	(have) drawn
drink	drank	(have) drunk
eat	ate	(have) eaten
fly	flew	(have) flown
give	gave	(have) given
go	went	(have) gone
have	had	(have) had
keep	kept	(have) kept
know	knew	(have) known
make	made	(have) made
ride	rode	(have) ridden
run	ran	(have) run
say	said	(have) said
see	saw	(have) seen
sing	sang	(have) sung
sit	sat	(have) sat
speak	spoke	(have) spoken
swim	swam	(have) swum
take	took	(have) taken
tell	told	(have) told
think	thought	(have) thought
throw	threw	(have) thrown
wear	wore	(have) worn

Sing-Sang-Sung

If a song is sing-sang-sung,
why can't a gift be bring-brang-brung?
And if punch can be drink-drank-drunk,
why can't a thought be think-thank-thunk?
If birds take off and fly-flew-flown,
why don't sleeping dogs lie-lew-lown?

Storybook Game

Finish the sentence with the past participle form of the verb.
Clue: Think what the fairy-tale character would say.

Alice in Wonderland: "I _____ in my tears for the last time!" (swim)

Cinderella: "My stepsisters _____ to the ball." (go)

Sleeping Beauty: "The fairy godmothers _____ my location a secret." (keep)

Pinocchio's father, Geppetto: "You should _____ you can't tell a lie!" (know)

Answers are on page 57.

BRAIN GAMES

Finish the Rhymes

Finish these rhymes using the correct verb part.

1. I _____ a song, (sing—future)
   Though not very long,
   Yet I _____ it as pretty as any. (think—present)
   _____ your hand in your purse (put—present)
   You _____ never _____ worse, (be—future)
   And _____ the poor singer a penny. (give—present)

2. There _____ a crooked man, who walked a crooked mile,
   (be—past)
   He _____ a crooked sixpence against a crooked stile. (find—past)
   He _____ a crooked cat, which _____ a crooked mouse
   (buy, catch—past)
   And they all lived together in a crooked little house.

Answers are on page 57.

Making Subjects and Verbs Agree

When subjects and verbs seek partners...

> **Subject:** How do you do? I'm singular.
> **Verb:** Oh, dear. I'm afraid I'm plural.
> **Subject:** Too bad! We can never agree. It just wouldn't work.
> **Verb:** No. Sorry. Nice meeting you anyway.

I DIDN'T KNOW VERBS COULD COUNT!

Remember that nouns may be singular or plural. A singular noun names one person, place, or thing. A plural noun names two or more people, places, or things.

Singular	Plural
a pet	many pets
one grandma	both my grandmas

Now hear this! Verbs can be singular or plural, too. When you write a sentence, the subject and verb must agree in number. This means a singular verb goes with a singular subject:

> A pet makes you happy.
> My grandma reads stories to me.

A plural verb goes with a plural subject:

> Many pets make you happy. Both my grandmas read stories to me.

Singular nouns do not have an -s, so they need a partner verb with an -s. Plural nouns do have an -s, so they look for a partner verb that has no -s.

Exception: When the subject is *I* or *you*, do not add an -s to the verb. Use the base form as the singular:

> I love animals. You like them, too, don't you?

The *be* verbs have different singular and plural forms in both present and past tense.

Singular	Plural
He is my friend.	They are my friends.
She was late.	They were late.

Slipups

Fooler Phrases

Be sure you find the real subject of the sentence. Sometimes a phrase comes between the subject and the verb. Do not be fooled. The verb should agree with the subject, not necessarily the nearest noun.

> The *spices* in the food *are* tasty. ("Spices" is the subject, not "food.")
>
> *One* of my friends *likes* hot peppers. ("One" is the subject, not "friends.")

CHECKUP ✔

Be Agreeable!

Which verb agrees with the subject in number? Circle the subject of each sentence. Decide if it is singular or plural. Then write the verb that agrees with the subject in the blank.

1. A holiday with grandparents _____ special. (is/are)

2. I _____ having them come for my birthday. (love/loves)

3. Grandma always _____ me a hug. (give/gives)

4. Grandpa always _____, "My, how you have grown!" (say/says)

5. Dad _____ me a chocolate cake. (bake/bakes)

6. Mom _____ my presents in funny papers. (wrap/wraps)

7. The candles on my cake _____ pretty. (look/looks)

8. My parents _____ me stay up late. (let/lets)

9. The train with a whistle and bells _____ my favorite. (is/are)

10. Birthdays _____ the greatest! (is/are)

Answers are on page 57.

ANSWERS

page 38

PHYSICAL OR MENTAL ACTION?
Sample answers: yelled (physical), chased (physical), wagged (physical), thought (mental), wanted (mental)

page 40

CHECKUP
Sample answers: 1) sweet, describe; 2) salty, describe; 3) teacher, identify; 4) farmer, identify; 5) butterfly, identify; 6) beautiful, describe

page 41

MAKING CONNECTIONS
1) am; 2) are; 3) is; 4) looks; 5) seems; 6) sounds; 7) feels

page 42

DIRECTOR OF DIRECT OBJECTS
Sample answers: Mary, soccer ball, soccer, a snack

page 43

CHECKUP
Jim *found* (*) a strange animal. It *looked* (✓) very odd. He said, "Maybe it *is* (✓) a worm." But it *had* (✓) legs. Its shell *felt* (✓) hard. Then he *gave* (*) it a poke. The thing *rolled* (*) itself into a ball. "I *will call* (*) you Roly-Poly," said Jim.

page 45

STORY COMPLETION
was sleeping, was swinging, must have thought, had sprung, was attached, do/get

page 47

CHECKUP
Dear Grandma and Grandpa,
How *are* you? I *hope* you feel fine. Right now, I *am* very wet. That is because Daddy and I just *washed* the dog. It *was* quite a show.

Pluto *shook* as though he was freezing. In fact, the water *was* warm. When we put on the shampoo, he *hung* his head. He seemed to be saying, "Why *are* you punishing me?" Then we *rinsed* him off. He was so happy to be out of the tub, he *wagged* his whole body while we *dried* him.

page 49

TIMING IS EVERYTHING
1) The cherry trees have been in bloom (all spring). 2) I have written stories and poems (for years). 3) The team has played well (this season).

page 51

HOW PROGRESSIVE ARE YOU?
1) is taking; 2) are climbing; 3) was teaching; 4) had been playing; 5) are learning; 6) will be teaching

page 54

CHECKUP
Alice in Wonderland: have swum
Cinderella: have gone
Sleeping Beauty: have kept
Pinocchio's father, Geppetto: have known

FINISH THE RHYMES
1. will sing, think, Put, will/be, give
2. was, found, bought, caught

page 56

CHECKUP
1. holiday, is
2. I, love
3. Grandma, gives
4. Grandpa, says
5. Dad, bakes
6. Mom, wraps
7. candles, look
8. parents, let
9. train, is
10. Birthdays, are

Pronouns
Words That Replace Nouns

What are *they?* Without pronouns, there would be no *you* or *me.*

What Is a Pronoun?

Yes, *what* can be a pronoun. Many other words are pronouns, too. Take a look at these sentences. You'll find all kinds of pronouns. *Pronouns* can pop up almost anywhere in a sentence.

Tracy and she practiced on the balance beam.

You should try this new computer card game.

Bob gave him a remote-control airplane for his birthday. Everybody had fun flying it.

Some pronouns, like *she, you,* and *him,* refer to a specific person or thing. Some pronouns, like *his,* show possession. All these are called *personal pronouns.* Other pronouns, such as *everybody,* do not refer to a specific person or thing. They are called *indefinite pronouns.*

Personal Pronouns

Personal pronouns take the place of nouns in sentences. Do you know what pronouns to choose in the following paragraph? Go ahead and choose.

Juan told (I, me) it was (his, her) birthday. (They, I) said, "(You, He) must be kidding! (I, You) wish I had known." (They, We) finished walking to my house. "(You, He) might as well come in," (you, I) said. (They, We) walked in. "Surprise!" everyone shouted. (Me, I) wish you could have seen Juan's face. (He, She) was completely surprised.

You were probably able to pick the correct pronouns. That is because you use pronouns every day. You usually do not have to think about which pronoun to use. But there are some rules. The rules tell you which personal pronouns to use.

The form of the personal pronoun changes. Its form depends on whether the noun it refers to is:

first person, second person, or third person
male, female, or neither
singular or plural
used as a subject or an object in a sentence

YOU STAYS THE SAME

This chart shows personal pronouns.

Personal Pronouns			
	Singular Subject	Singular Object	Plural Subject	Plural Object
First Person	I	me	we	us
Second Person	you	you	you	you
Third Person	he, she, it	him, her, it	they	them

BRAIN GAMES

You Call Me

The following words are written in a telephone code. To break the code, look at the numbers on a telephone key pad. Each number key has three letters. Find the letters that correspond to the numbers of each coded word below. Figure out which letters spell a pronoun. Write each pronoun.

1. 8 4 3 9   3. 7 4 3   5. 6 3
2. 4   4. 9 6 8

Are You Stopping Here?

The following joke contains 10 pronouns that refer to people. Can you find them all?

A man went to see his doctor. "Dr. Fishman," he said, "what should I do? My wife thinks she is an elevator."

"Tell her to come see me," Dr. Fishman said.

"She can't," the man said. "She doesn't stop at your floor."

Answers are on page 72.

Personal Choice

I, YOU, OR THEM

A writer decides whom the story is about. Maybe a writer wants to tell about his own life. Then he would use the style of *first person*—that is the person speaking. Maybe a writer wants to talk directly to the reader. She would use *second person*—the person spoken to. Perhaps a writer wants to tell about what happened to someone. The writer would use *third person*—the person, place, or thing spoken about.

> Jamal went to the movies. He paid for the ticket. Then he had to choose from several films that were showing. He settled on an action flick and bought popcorn and soda.

Did you notice that the story is focused on Jamal all the way through? It is written in third person.

Take a look at the next paragraph. In which person is the story written?

> Beth, Kim, and Theo went to the beach Saturday. You can do lots of fun things at the beach. People surf, swim, and jet ski. You can even rent a kayak. On the sand, I have enjoyed lots of activities. You can build sand castles, go for walks, and play ball games. Beth and Kim sat on the sand. Theo played volleyball.

Are you a bit confused? The paragraph begins in third person. It describes Beth, Kim, and Theo. But soon it changes into second person—*you*—and then into first person—*I*. It does not make sense because it is not consistent in person.

You may use more than one pronoun person in a paragraph. The following paragraph is told in first person. But it still refers to others, using third person.

> I went to the beach Saturday. I saw Beth, Kim, and Theo there. They were playing on the sand.

The first beach story starts in third person. The second beach story starts in first person. Decide which person you are using. Then be consistent. You always tell a story in either first person or third person. Because you only tell stories about yourself or someone else, you rarely write stories in second person.

BRAIN GAMES

Who's in the Band?

The following paragraph starts with third person. Then it shifts. Revise the paragraph. Use third person consistently.

> Jody and Brendan started a band. Jody played the guitar, and Brendan played drums. You can play lots of songs with these two instruments. Soon they recruited Eva, who played the piano. I know a lot of great songs that include the piano. The three of them practiced in Jody's basement for weeks. You should have heard them in the school talent show.

Answers are on page 72.

Using Subject and Object Pronouns

WE AND *HE* VERSUS *HIM* AND *THEM*

"Me want cookie!"

You have probably heard a famous puppet character say this many times. Of course, you would never use the pronoun *me* this way. But maybe you have said something like this:

> Terry and him went on the roller coaster four times.

Oops! Something is wrong here. This sentence needs a *subject pronoun*.

> Terry and he went on the roller coaster four times.

You can avoid this kind of mistake. You just need to know the difference between subject pronouns and object pronouns.

SUBJECT PRONOUNS
I See
When a pronoun is the subject of a sentence, use a subject pronoun: *I, you, he, she, it, we, they*. (Flip back to the Personal Pronouns chart on page 59 to review.) In each sentence below, a *subject pronoun* is the subject.

> Yesterday we went to the fair.
> I saw Simple Simon there.
> He was selling all kinds of wares.

Sometimes a sentence has a compound subject. If a compound subject includes a pronoun, always use a subject pronoun.

> Sam and I looked up at the stars.
> The moon and they were shining.

You can check by seeing if the subject pronoun works alone:

> I looked up at the stars.

OBJECT PRONOUNS
Advice for *You*

The *object pronouns* are *me, you, him, her, it, us, them.* (See the chart on page 59.) Only object pronouns can be used as the object of a verb in a sentence.

> The motorboat pulled him.
> The water-skier impressed us.

Object pronouns are also used as the objects of prepositions. A *preposition* is a word that relates a noun or pronoun to another word in the sentence. The noun or pronoun that follows the preposition (such as *by* or *to*) is called the *object of the preposition.* (You will learn more about prepositions in Chapter 7.)

> The class read a story by Ben.
> The class read a story by him.
> Its ending was a surprise to them.

Choose the correct pronoun to complete each sentence.

1. Tracy's favorite musicians were playing, and she wanted to see (they, them).
2. Another band and (them, they) were performing at City Auditorium.
3. Brooke and (I, me) wanted to go too.
4. Tracy's dad knew the band's manager, so he called (she, her).
5. The band played (we, us) a special song.

Answers are on page 72.

Possessive Pronouns

TAKE POSSESSION!

You make it yours when it is possessive.

What is your favorite kind of movie? Mine is animation. My second favorite is fantasy. Henry is a huge movie fan. His favorite kind of movie is science fiction. What's yours?

The highlighted words above are *possessive pronouns*. Possessive pronouns are special personal pronouns. You know that sometimes nouns show possession. You can replace possessive nouns with possessive pronouns:

Anita's baseball mitt	her baseball mitt
the Franklins' yard	their yard
the cat's fur	its fur

Here are the possessive pronouns.

Possessive Pronouns

	Singular	Plural
First Person	my, mine	our, ours
Second Person	your, yours	your, yours
Third Person	his, her, hers, its	their, theirs

BRAIN GAMES

Independence Day

Can you find all the possessive pronouns in this paragraph about the Fourth of July? Underline each of them.

My favorite holiday is the Fourth of July. Our town has a huge parade. All of its bands, horses, and antique cars are on display. This year my mom made a fruit salad. Hers had blue and red berries in it as well as bananas and other fruit. My little brother was so excited because he won his race. Seeing the fireworks is my favorite part of the celebration. The fireworks show is amazing. Every year, its lights and noises seem bigger, brighter, and louder. I can't wait for our next Independence Day!

Answers are on page 72.

Slipups

Its versus It's

Don't confuse the words *its* and *it's*. Possessive pronouns do not use apostrophes. The possessive form of *it is its*, without an apostrophe. The word *it's* is a contraction, a shortened way of writing *it is*.

> The dog had mud on its coat. — possessive

> It's wet outside. — contraction of *it is*

Choose the correct word for each sentence.

1. Brian and (his, him) dad arrived at the stadium early.
2. It was nearly empty when (they, their) sat down.
3. They watched as players took (them, their) practice swings.
4. Brian had (his, him) baseball mitt with (his, him).
5. He hoped to catch a ball with (him, it).

Answers are on page 73.

Indefinite Pronouns

NOTHING PERSONAL

Michelle and her family were walking around Portland. They didn't know their way around.

"Excuse me," Michelle said to a person walking by. "Where is the harbor?"

"Everybody knows that!" said the person.

Michelle decided to ask another person.

"Anybody can tell you that!" said the second person.

Now Michelle was getting a little upset. Still, she asked another person.

"Somebody can tell you that," said the third person.

Michelle wondered why nobody would help them.

How would you feel if you were Michelle? *Everybody, anybody,* and *somebody* could help...but *nobody* did! All these pronouns refer to some general person. They are *indefinite pronouns.* Unlike the personal pronouns *I, she,* and *him* that refer to a specific person, indefinite pronouns refer to someone or something that is not specific.

Here is a list of indefinite pronouns.

Indefinite Pronouns

all	neither
any	nobody
anybody	none
anyone	no one
anything	nothing
each	one
either	some
everybody	somebody
everyone	someone
everything	something

CHECKUP ✔

Complete each sentence with an indefinite pronoun.

1. _____ wanted to give Ms. Snyder a going-away party.

2. _____ except Tony and Ally volunteered.

3. On the day of the party, _____ went wrong.

4. _____ of the snacks turned out right.

5. Still, _____ enjoyed the party.

Answers are on page 73.

Some Other Kinds of Pronouns

REFLEXIVE PRONOUNS

Have you ever boasted, "I did it myself"? You used a reflexive pronoun: *myself*. *Reflexive pronouns* are formed when you add *-self* or *-selves* to some personal pronouns. We use these pronouns to add emphasis or to refer back to who did something.

> Toby made the prizes for the party himself.—*himself* emphasizes that Toby made the prizes.

> The children helped themselves to prizes.—*themselves* refers back to the children.

This chart shows reflexive pronouns.

Slipups

Subjects Lack Self
Reflexive pronouns cannot be subjects. Never use a pronoun that ends in *-self* or *-selves* alone as the subject of a sentence.

Incorrect: Wendy and myself rode in a hot-air balloon.

Correct: Wendy and I rode in a hot-air balloon.

Reflexive Pronouns

	Singular	Plural
First Person	myself	ourselves
Second Person	yourself	yourselves
Third Person	himself, herself, itself	themselves

INTERROGATIVE PRONOUNS
What Is the Question?

If you were a newspaper reporter, you would be using lots of interrogative pronouns. Interrogative pronouns ask questions. These pronouns are *who, whom, whose, which,* and *what.*

> Who solved the mystery of the haunted mansion?
> Which characters did you suspect?
> What was the clue?

Why do owls make good newspaper reporters?

They are always asking, "Who?"

BRAIN GAMES

Proverbs with Pronouns

Each sentence on the left is a popular saying that is missing a word.
Complete each saying with a pronoun on the right.

1. To make friends, be _____.

2. _____ am the master of my fate.

3. _____ you can do, I can do better.

4. _____ great was ever achieved without enthusiasm.

A. nothing

B. yourself

C. anything

D. I

Answers are on page 73.

Pronouns and Antecedents

WHAT COMES BEFORE?

The word *antecedent* comes from a
Latin word meaning "to go before."
A personal pronoun needs an
antecedent so it won't be
misunderstood. What are the
antecedents of the pronouns in these
sentences?

> Kathleen said she would feed the
> newborn baby panda.

> Chimpanzees play when they feel good.

In the first sentence, the antecedent of the pronoun *she* is *Kathleen*. That means
the pronoun *she* refers back to the noun *Kathleen. Kathleen* tells us who *she* is.
Kathleen "goes before" *she*. In the second sentence, what is the antecedent of
they? In other words, what noun does the pronoun *they* refer to? *They* refers to
chimpanzees. The antecedent of *they* is *chimpanzees*.

CHECKUP ✔

Write the antecedent of each underlined pronoun in the sentences below.

1. Lily said cheetahs are <u>her</u> favorite kind of cat.
2. The legs of a cheetah are long compared to <u>its</u> body.
3. Most cheetahs make <u>their</u> home in Africa.
4. Mr. Ryan said that cheetahs can go as fast as <u>his</u> car.
5. To keep up with Mr. Ryan, the animal must run at <u>its</u> top speed of 70 miles per hour.

Answers are on page 73.

Don't Be Disagreeable

You've heard of disagreements between friends, sisters and brothers, business partners, and even countries. But disagreements between pronouns?

It's not that pronouns exactly disagree. But you must always make sure the pronouns you use do agree. Pronouns must agree with their antecedents in several different ways:

> in person
> in gender
> in number

A pronoun must also agree in number with its verb. Whew! That's a lot of agreement. (See Pronoun/Verb Agreement on page 71.)

Pronoun/Antecedent Agreement

When you use a pronoun in a sentence or a paragraph, make sure it agrees with its antecedent in *person.*

> Chad and Louis hope they can climb Mount Everest in a few years.

This sentence is written in third person. It refers not to me or you but to two other people. The pronoun in the sentence must also be in third person. The pronoun *they* is a third-person pronoun.

Sharon took off her shoes and jumped on her trampoline.

When you write a sentence or a paragraph that includes pronouns, you must make sure they agree with their antecedent in *gender*. In the sentence above, Sharon is a girl. So the possessive pronoun in the sentence must be the singular possessive pronoun *her* that refers to a girl.

Brittany and I got our puppy from the animal shelter.

The subject *Brittany and I* includes more than one person. So the number of the subject is plural. You must use a plural pronoun to agree with the plural subject. The first-person plural pronoun *our* agrees with the plural subject. So the pronouns agree in *number*.

Agreement with Indefinite Pronouns

"NO ONE ATE HIS OR HER VEGETABLES"

Everybody goes to the movies on Friday night.
No one is taking his or her friends to see the new movie.

Look at the first sentence above. The subject is the indefinite pronoun *everybody*. The verb *goes* is the singular form of the verb *go*. It agrees with the pronoun *everybody*, which is also singular. In the second sentence, *no one* is the antecedent of *his/her*. Because *no one* is singular, any noun or pronoun that refers to it must also be singular. *His* and *her* are singular pronouns.

Indefinite pronouns that are always singular:

anybody	neither
anyone	nobody
anything	no one
each	nothing
either	one
everybody	somebody
everyone	someone
everything	something

When one of these pronouns is the antecedent of another pronoun, the pronoun must be singular.

Each brings his own bat to practice.

In this sentence, the singular indefinite pronoun *each* is the antecedent of the singular pronoun *his*. Indefinite pronouns often refer to both boys and girls. For example, your teacher might say,

"Can someone describe his or her favorite part of the story?"

In this sentence, the compound pronoun *his or her* is singular. It agrees with its singular antecedent, *someone*. Also, it refers to people of both genders. It includes both boys and girls.

In the sentences below, the pronouns agree in number with their antecedents, which are indefinite pronouns.

Does anybody have his or her umbrella?
Everyone must bring his or her sleeping bag.

You may be tempted to say, "No one ate their vegetables." When you are chatting with your friends and family, this is fine. Also, there are sometimes ways to avoid using "his or her." For example, you could say, "No one ate the vegetables." But when you write or speak formally, make sure the pronouns you use agree correctly with indefinite pronouns.

BRAIN GAMES

Getting Everyone Into the Act

Everyone can imagine the excitement of having a film crew in town. Read the paragraph below. Some of the sentences have indefinite pronouns as their subjects. Check to see if all the pronouns agree with their antecedents. Revise sentences with faulty pronoun agreement.

Has anybody ever come to your town to make their movie? Last week some famous actors came to Greenville. Everybody has seen them on their TV. Everyone in town took their cameras to the location. Nothing happened for a long time. Everybody talked to their neighbors. Finally the actors appeared. The director called for action and then stopped.

The director asked the crowd, "Does somebody have their cell phone on?" Each person checked their purses and pockets. Then the filming began.

Answers are on page 73.

Pronoun/Verb Agreement

I go to the skate park.
You go to the skate park.
He goes to the skate park.

Look at the verbs and subjects. You know that they must agree in number. Sometimes a pronoun is the subject of a sentence. A singular pronoun takes the singular form of a verb. A plural pronoun takes the plural form of a verb.

The following chart shows the present tense form of the verb "to be" that you should use with each subject pronoun.

Pronoun Subjects and "to be"

	Singular	Plural
First Person	I am	we are
Second Person	you are	you are
Third Person	he is, she is, it is	they are

BRAIN GAMES

Do You Have a License for that Pronoun?

It's time for some fun with pronouns. You've seen car license plates that spell out a message. They are often called vanity plates. The vanity plates below have messages that use shortened forms of pronouns and other words. Write out each license plate. Underline each pronoun.

1. R U BZ   _____

2. I M A DJ   _____

3. U KN XL   _____

4. U TK IT EZ   _____

5. I M 8E   _____

Answers are on page 73.

Circle the verb that correctly completes each sentence.

1. Everyone on our block (has, have) a favorite form of transportation.

2. We (ride, rides) our scooters everywhere.

3. Olivia and he (prefer, prefers) skateboards.

4. Mr. Jenks has an unusual way of walking. He (like, likes) snowshoes.

5. Of course, nobody (get, gets) far on snowshoes in June.

Answers are on page 73.

Answers

page 59

YOU CALL ME
1. they
2. I
3. she
4. you
5. me

ARE YOU STOPPING HERE?
his, he, I, my, she, her, me, she, she, your

page 61

WHO'S IN THE BAND?
(Answers can vary.)
Jody and Brendan started a band. Jody played the guitar, and Brendan played drums. They found they could play lots of songs with these two instruments. Soon they recruited Eva, who played the piano. A lot of great songs include the piano. The three of them practiced in Jody's basement for weeks. Soon they performed in the school talent show.

page 62

CHECKUP
1. them
2. they
3. I
4. her
5. us

page 63

INDEPENDENCE DAY
My favorite holiday is the Fourth of July. Our town has a huge parade. All of its bands, horses, and antique cars are on display. This year my mom made a fruit salad. Hers had blue and red berries in it as well as bananas and other fruit. My little brother was so excited because he won his race. Seeing the fireworks is my favorite part of the celebration. The fireworks show is amazing. Every year, its lights and noises seem bigger, brighter, and louder. I can't wait for our next Independence Day!

page 64

CHECKUP
1. his
2. they
3. their
4. his, him
5. it

page 65

CHECKUP
(Answers can vary.)
1. Everyone
2. Nobody
3. everything
4. None
5. everyone

page 67

PROVERBS WITH PRONOUNS
1. B
2. D
3. C
4. A

page 68

CHECKUP
1. Lily
2. cheetah
3. cheetahs
4. Mr. Ryan
5. animal

page 70

GETTING EVERYONE INTO THE ACT
Has anybody ever come to your town to make *a* movie? Last week some famous actors came to Greenville. Everybody has seen them on *his or her* TV. Everyone in town took *a camera* to the location. Nothing happened for a long time. Everybody talked to *his or her* neighbors. Finally the actors appeared. The director called for action and then stopped.

The director asked the crowd, "Does somebody have *a* cell phone on?" Each person checked *his or her* purse and pockets. Then the filming began.

page 71

DO YOU HAVE A LICENSE FOR THAT PRONOUN?
1. Are <u>you</u> busy?
2. <u>I</u> am a DJ (disc jockey).
3. <u>You</u> can excel.
4. <u>You</u> take <u>it</u> easy.
5. <u>I</u> am eighty.

page 72

CHECKUP
1. has
2. ride
3. prefer
4. likes
5. gets

Adjectives
A Spicy Part of Speech

These descriptive words add interest and flavor to simple sentences.

Adjectives describe people, places, and things. They add spice to a sentence. Read the two vacation stories below.

> Near the beach is a hotel. The grounds are filled with plants. The restaurant serves snacks and drinks. Kids and adults enjoy activities on the beach and in the water.

> Near the sparkling white beach is a luxurious hotel. The private grounds are filled with lush tropical plants and bright flowers. The casual outdoor restaurant serves tasty snacks and refreshing drinks. Kids and adults enjoy fun, thrilling activities on the glittering beach and in the gentle, warm water.

What's the difference between the first vacation spot and the second one? Adjectives! Adjectives can turn a boring vacation spot into an inviting one.

Tricks
Two huge green old monsters!

Sometimes you use two adjectives in a row to describe a noun. Sometimes you put a comma between the adjectives. Sometimes you don't. Here's the rule of thumb: Usually you do not need a comma if the adjective tells about size, shape, age, color, or number.

big silver alien   ten white birds   new round pool

Adjectives answer the following questions about nouns and pronouns:

Which one?	this game, that car, those mountains
What kind?	pretty cat, fresh milk, American ship
How many?	some computers, seven miles, several days
How much?	enough food, less rain, more time

Adjectives can show up in any part of a sentence. Sometimes they are in the complete subject of a sentence.

> The tricky new game fascinated people. — The adjectives *tricky* and *new* describe the subject *game*.

> A bright rainbow appeared. — The adjective *bright* describes the subject *rainbow*.

Sometimes adjectives are in the complete predicate of a sentence.

> The mansion looks huge and mysterious. — The adjectives *huge* and *mysterious* are in the predicate. They describe the subject *mansion*.

> She is calm and patient. — The adjectives *calm* and *patient* describe the subject *she*.

> Keesha fed the thin, hungry animal. — The adjectives *thin* and *hungry* describe the direct object *animal*.

Wherever they appear, adjectives always describe, or modify, nouns or pronouns.

Some adjectives end in *-ing* or *-ed*. Don't confuse these with verbs (such as *walking* or *walked*). If they describe a noun or a pronoun, they are adjectives.

> The new puppy is charming yet annoying. — The adjectives *charming* and *annoying* describe the noun *puppy*.

> The taped note said to meet at the treehouse. — The adjective *taped* describes the noun *note*.

CHECKUP ✔

Find each adjective in the following sentences. Tell what question each one answers about its noun or pronoun.

1. That national park includes tall mountains and ancient forests.
2. Many people camp out near the thundering waterfall.
3. Some campers sleep near the immense ocean.
4. They can hear the soft barks of sea lions during cool nights.
5. The wild animals are beautiful and unusual.

Answers are on page 85.

BRAIN GAMES

Hink Pinks

A "Hink Pink" is a riddle with an answer of two rhyming words that are synonyms for words in the riddle. The answer words are usually an adjective and a noun. Here's an example:

> What do you call a race for pleasure? A fun run.

1. What do you call someone who likes to lay out in the sun? A _____ fan

2. What do you call a long, thin, rubber animal without legs? A _____ snake

3. What do you call a chair that is made out of rock? A _____ throne

4. What do you call a bowl you put guppies in? A _____ dish

5. What do you call rodents that say "please" and "thank you"? _____ mice

Answers are on page 85.

Predicate Adjectives

DESCRIBING THE SUBJECT OF A SENTENCE

A predicate adjective is linked by the verb to the subject.

Subject **I** → Linking Verb **am** → Predicate Adjective **smart**

What would you say if someone asked you to describe yourself? You might say, "I am funny" or "I am tall." When you complete the sentence "I am…" with an adjective, you are using a predicate adjective. The verb *am* is a linking verb. Linking verbs link the subject of a sentence to an adjective or a noun in the predicate.

Each sentence below has a *predicate adjective.* Each one follows a linking verb. The predicate adjective describes the subject of the sentence.

> The mother cat acts gentle.
> The new kitten feels soft.
> Our puppy is jealous of the new kitten.

Adjectives can describe other words in a predicate. For example, in the third sentence, the word *new* is an adjective but not a predicate adjective. That is because *new* describes *kitten*, which is not the subject of the sentence. To be a predicate adjective, an adjective must follow a linking verb and describe the subject of the sentence.

What did the river say to the canyon?

¡uoʎuɐɔ puɐɹ⅁ ɐ ǝɹ,noʎ

CHECKUP

Underline each predicate adjective in the sentences. A sentence may have more than one predicate adjective.

1. Antarctica is icy and frigid.
2. It is perfect for penguins, though.
3. Penguins appear happy here.
4. Penguins look sophisticated.
5. They seem ready for a fancy ball.

Answers are on page 85.

BRAIN GAMES

Cartoon Characters Are Colorful, Crazy, and Comical

Underline each predicate adjective in the paragraph.

Cartoon characters are fun. They have entertaining personalities. Some are friendly. Others are sassy. A few are unusual. A certain cartoon boy is annoying but lovable. Who is your favorite character?

Answers are on page 85.

Proper Adjectives

WHAT ARE FRENCH, MARTIAN, AND CALIFORNIAN?

Anton comes from France.
Anton is a French citizen.

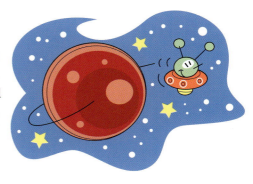

Proper nouns name a specific person, place, or thing. They begin with a capital letter. A *proper adjective* is made from a proper noun. It also begins with a capital letter. In the sentence above, *French* is a proper adjective. (It is made from the proper noun *France*.) It describes the noun *citizen*. Here are more proper adjectives:

American sport   Shakespearean play   Martian atmosphere

We already know that sometimes nouns are used as adjectives.

chemistry test   tennis game   pet shop

Proper nouns can be used as adjectives, too.

California highway   New York restaurant   Florida beach

CHECKUP ✔

Capitalize each proper adjective in the following sentences.

1. Jill's new dog is an irish setter.
2. Jeffrey rides an arabian horse at his ranch.
3. Does a persian cat or a siamese cat have longer hair?
4. That huge cat is an indian tiger.
5. An african elephant has bigger ears than an asian elephant.

Answers are on page 85.

BRAIN GAMES

International Party

Revise the following letter. Replace each phrase naming a country with a phrase that uses a proper adjective.

Dear Gran,

    Our class is having an international party. Everyone has to bring a food from the country the teacher assigned. Bobby is bringing tacos, a spicy dish from Mexico. Jen is making a trifle, a fancy dessert from England. Stephanie will bring spaghetti, everyone's favorite food from Italy. Daniel's mom is making borscht, a soup from Russia. I'm not telling what country I have. I just have one question. What is a tasty, exciting dish from Canada?

    Your grandson,

    Mick

Answers are on page 85.

Articles

LITTLE ADJECTIVES THAT MAKE A BIG DIFFERENCE

"Brown bear broke into apartment and ate box of doughnuts."

Hmmm. You can understand this sentence, but it sounds funny. What's missing? Three little words: *a, an, the*

    The brown bear broke into an apartment and ate a box of doughnuts.

A, an, and *the* are special adjectives. They are called *articles.* Like other adjectives, they modify nouns. They are the most common adjectives in English.

The article *the* is called a *definite article.* It refers to specific persons, places, or things. It may be used with a singular noun or a plural noun.

    the hippos in the watering hole
    the hippo on the shore

The articles *a* and *an* are called *indefinite articles.* Each refers to a noun that is one of many of its kind. Use them only before singular nouns. Use the article *a* before words that begin with a consonant sound. Use the article *an* before words that begin with a vowel sound.

> an anteater   an upset hippo
> a hippo   a giraffe

Write the correct article—*a, an,* or *the*—for each blank.

1. Did you ever want to be _____ knight in shining armor?

2. A knight's job was to protect _____ kingdom.

3. Every knight wore _____ heavy suit of armor.

4. _____ armor suit could weigh 55 pounds.

5. _____ knights might be away from home for _____ long time.

6. You would not call _____ meals they had to eat very tasty.

7. _____ meal might be _____ moldy biscuit.

8. A knight's meal might also include _____ uncooked piece of meat.

9. This does not sound like _____ easy life.

10. Maybe you would not want to be _____ knight after all.

Answers are on page 85.

Demonstrative Adjectives

DISCUSSING *THIS* AND *THAT*

This player scores a lot of goals. That player is a great goalie. These players practice every day. Those players have won every game.

The words *this, that, these,* and *those* are *demonstrative adjectives.* They answer the question *which one?* about the nouns they modify. How do you know whether to use *this, that, these,* or *those?*

Imagine yourself pointing to an object such as a flag. *This* flag and *these* flags are usually nearby. *That* flag and *those* flags are farther away. Also remember that you use the words *this* and *that* with singular nouns. You use the words *these* and *those* with plural nouns.

BRAIN GAMES

This and These

Add a demonstrative adjective to each blank in the paragraph.

_____ facts are about two favorite foods. In the 1700s, there lived an English noble named John Montagu, the Earl of Sandwich. _____ noble wanted a quick snack: He put meat between bread slices and made the first sandwich. In Germany, sausages are called frankfurters. _____ sausages were first made in the city of Frankfurt. An American named them "hot dogs." He first called _____ sausages "hot dachshund sausages." Can you see why?

Answers are on page 85.

Using Adjectives to Compare

POSITIVE, COMPARATIVE, OR SUPERLATIVE?
Superlative is the highest you can go!

Where would the judges at a dog show be without adjectives? They must compare many dogs, so they use comparative forms of adjectives. The judges have opinions about each dog. Listen in.

> Judge 1: Pierre is sweet.
> Judge 2: But Max is smarter.
> Judge 1: Flossy is cutest.

There are three degrees of comparative adjectives:

Positive Degree	Comparative Degree	Superlative Degree
fast	faster	fastest
tasty	tastier	tastiest
slim	slimmer	slimmest

The *positive degree* is the regular form of an adjective. You use it when you are describing one noun. This is the form you find when you look up an adjective in the dictionary.

The Popsicle™ is tasty.

You use the *comparative degree* of an adjective to compare two things. Look at the adjectives in the list above. To make the comparative form of many adjectives like these, add -*er* to the positive degree.

The apple pie is tastier than the Popsicle™.

Sometimes to change a positive adjective to a comparative adjective, you change the spelling of the word. When an adjective ends in *y*, you change the *y* to *i* before adding -*er*. *Tasty* becomes *tastier*. When a one-syllable word ends in a consonant, you usually double the consonant before adding -*er*. The word *slim* becomes *slimmer*.

You use the *superlative degree* when you compare three or more things. To make the superlative form of many adjectives, you add -*est* to the positive degree.

Of the three desserts, the hot fudge sundae is tastiest.

Sometimes you need to change the spelling of the positive form to make it superlative. You just did this for the comparative form. When an adjective ends in *y*, you change the *y* to *i* before adding -*est*. *Tasty* becomes *tastiest*. When a one-syllable word ends in a consonant, you usually double the consonant before adding -*est*. *Slim* becomes *slimmest*.

BRAIN GAMES

Hink Pinks—It's All Comparative

Finish these Hink Pinks. The adjective is in the comparative degree. Think of a comparative adjective that rhymes with each noun.

1. What do you call a wetter laundry bin? _____ hamper

2. What do you call a slimmer champ? _____ winner

3. What do you call a more bashful pilot? _____ flyer

4. What do you call a thinner washer? _____ cleaner

5. What do you call a more ancient rock? _____ boulder

Answers are on page 85.

CHECKUP ✓

Underline each adjective. (You do not need to underline articles.) Tell whether each is in the positive, comparative, or superlative degree.

1. Snowboarding is one of the newer sports in the Olympics.

2. In an event called the halfpipe, young athletes do cool tricks on snowboards.

3. A halfpipe is a wide, snowy pit shaped like a U.

4. Snowboards for the halfpipe are wider than those for the giant slalom.

5. In the halfpipe, athletes do the craziest tricks, like the "roast beef grab" and the "air to fakie."

Answers are on page 85.

SOME MORE ADJECTIVES THAT COMPARE

You know how to use *-er* and *-est* to form the comparative and superlative of most one-syllable and two-syllable adjectives. But for many adjectives with two or more syllables, you form the comparative and superlative degrees differently.

My parrot Polly is talkative and alert.

To form the comparative degree of adjectives such as *talkative* and *alert*, you use the word *more* or *less*.

> My parrot Polly is more talkative and more alert than my neighbor's parrot.

To form the superlative degree of adjectives such as *talkative* and *alert*, you use the word *most* or *least*.

> My parrot Polly is the most talkative and the most alert parrot in the world.

Irregular Forms of Comparison

Jerry's young brother wants to make a point, but he's having a bit of trouble.

> Jerry is the goodest... Jerry is the most good... Jerry is a good brother.

You can see why Jerry's little brother might be confused about how to form the superlative degree of the adjective *good*. It doesn't follow the usual pattern. You can't add -*er* or -*est* to *good*. You can't put *more*, *most*, *less*, or *least* before it. *Good* is an irregular adjective. That means its comparative and superlative forms are entirely different words from its positive form.

Here are some irregular adjectives:

Positive Degree	Comparative Degree	Superlative Degree
good	better	best
bad	worse	worst
little	littler or less	littlest or least
many	more	most

Slipups
Too Superlative

Never use both *more* and -*er* or both *most* and -*est*.

> Incorrect: Today is *more sunnier* than yesterday.
> Correct: Today is *sunnier* than yesterday.

Answers

page 75

CHECKUP

1) That—which one; national—what kind; tall—what kind; ancient—what kind. 2) Many—how many; thundering—what kind. 3) Some—how many; immense—what kind. 4) soft—what kind; cool—what kind. 5) wild—what kind; beautiful—what kind; unusual—what kind

page 76

HINK PINKS

1) tan; 2) fake; 3) stone; 4) fish; 5) Nice

page 77

CHECKUP

1. Antarctica is <u>icy</u> and <u>frigid.</u>
2. It is <u>perfect</u> for penguins, though.
3. Penguins appear <u>happy</u> here.
4. Penguins look <u>sophisticated.</u>
5. They seem <u>ready</u> for a fancy ball.

CARTOON CHARACTERS

Cartoon characters are <u>fun</u>. They have entertaining personalities. Some are <u>friendly</u>. Others are <u>sassy</u>. A few are <u>unusual</u>. A certain cartoon boy is <u>annoying</u> but <u>lovable</u>. Who is your favorite character?

page 78

CHECKUP

1) Irish; 2) Arabian; 3) Persian, Siamese; 4) Indian; 5) African, Asian

page 79

INTERNATIONAL PARTY

Dear Gran,

Our class is having an international party. Everyone has to bring a food from the country the teacher assigned. Bobby is bringing tacos, a spicy *Mexican dish.* Jen is making a trifle, a fancy *English dessert.* Stephanie will bring spaghetti, everyone's favorite *Italian food.* Daniel's mom is making borscht, a *Russian soup.* I'm not telling what country I have. I just have one question. What is a tasty, exciting *Canadian dish?*

Your grandson,
Mick

page 80

CHECKUP

1) a; 2) the; 3) a; 4) An or The; 5) The, a; 6) the; 7) A, a; 8) an; 9) an; 10) a

page 81

THIS AND THESE

These facts are about two favorite foods. In the 1700s, there lived an English noble named John Montagu, the Earl of Sandwich. *This* noble wanted a quick snack: He put meat between bread slices and made the first sandwich. In Germany, sausages are called frankfurters. *These* sausages were first made in the city of Frankfurt. An American named them "hot dogs." He first called *these* sausages "hot dachshund sausages." Can you see why?

page 83

HINK PINKS

1) damper; 2) thinner; 3) shyer; 4) leaner; 5) older

CHECKUP

1. newer—comparative
2. young—positive; cool—positive
3. wide—positive; snowy—positive
4. wider—comparative; giant—positive
5. craziest—superlative

Adverbs
Words with the Answers

An adverb tells about, or modifies, a verb, an adjective, or another adverb.

Adverbs answer the questions *how, when, where,* and *to what extent. To what extent* can tell us *how much* or *how long.*

Adverbs as Reporters

A good reporter knows the right questions. *How* did it happen? *When* did it happen? *Where* did it happen? Adverbs are something like reporters. They describe the action by telling how, when, and where.

The answers to *how, when, where,* and *to what extent* help us see the action of a story. Here's a tale that needs some adverbs:

The wind blew. Lightning struck a tree. The boy ran. He felt lucky.

For the story above, adverbs would help us see the action clearly:

The wind blew fiercely. —How did it blow? fiercely

Lightning struck a tree nearby. —Where did it strike? nearby

The boy ran home quickly. —Where did he run? home; how did he run? quickly

He felt very lucky. —To what extent did he feel lucky? very

Where the Action Is

Many adverbs tell us about verbs. They make the action more specific. In this sentence, which word tells how they fell? When they fell?

Mike and Bob fell hard yesterday.

You learned that adjectives tell about nouns and pronouns. Adjectives answer these questions about people, places, or things:

what kind?	loud noise
how many?	three parks
which one?	this morning

BRAIN GAMES

Adverb Sort

Make a chart with four columns labeled How? When? Where? To What Extent? Read the story below. The adverbs are underlined. Decide which question each adverb answers. Write the adverb under the question in the chart.

<u>Yesterday</u>, John and Maria <u>bravely</u> tried mountain climbing. They had <u>never</u> climbed anything steeper than a hill. They used <u>extremely</u> good equipment. They climbed <u>slowly</u> and <u>carefully</u>. They kept going <u>up</u>. The climb was <u>terribly</u> hard work. <u>Finally</u>, they reached the top!

"We did it!" said Maria <u>excitedly</u>.

"And to think," said John, "we <u>almost</u> backed out of the trip!"

Answers are on page 97.

THE -LY FAMILY

Many adjectives can be changed into adverbs. When you add *-ly*, an adjective that tells *what kind* becomes an adverb that tells *how*.

Adjective + -ly = Adverb

loud + -ly = loudly
happy + -ly = happily
sudden + -ly = suddenly
careful + -ly = carefully

For example, *a sudden storm* contains the adjective *sudden*. It tells what kind of storm. But *the storm came suddenly* contains the adverb *suddenly*. It tells how the storm came.

Slipups

Don't Count on "-ly" as a Clue

Many adverbs end in –ly. However, so do many adjectives:

an **early** train; a **friendly** person

To identify adverbs, ask yourself: What word does this word tell about? What question does it answer? If it tells about a verb, an adjective, or another adverb, it is an adverb. If it answers the question *how, when, where,* or *to what extent,* it is an adverb.

BRAIN GAMES

Very Punny

One kind of pun is a Tom Swiftie. These sentences have puns about what Tom is saying. For example, "I've never seen such flat land," Tom said *plainly.* Pick an adverb from the Word Bank to complete each sentence.

"You need to fix the tire," Tom said _____.

"The lemonade needs more sugar," Tom said _____.

"Come in from the rain," Tom said _____.

"The fire is going out," Tom said _____.

"Close the car windows," Tom said _____.

Word Bank				
breezily	coldly	dryly	flatly	tartly

Answers are on page 97.

Adverbs Get Around

Adverbs do not just add oomph to verbs. They can also tell more about adjectives. To describe something more clearly, add an adjective to an adverb.

> The lily pond was full of water. All the frogs were excited.

How full was the pond? How excited were the frogs? Adverbs can come to the rescue of these adjectives!

> The lily pond was completely full of water. All the frogs were quite excited.

In the last sentence, for example, *excited* is an adjective. It describes the noun *frogs.* How excited were they? Quite excited. *Quite* is an adverb that describes, or modifies, the adjective.

> The frogs slept on a very cozy lily pad.

In the sentence above, *cozy* is an adjective. It tells what kind of lily pad. *Very* tells to what extent the lily pad was cozy. *Very* is an adverb that modifies an adjective.

An adverb can make the adjective stronger. Compare these sentences:

> This cocoa is hot. —How hot is it? We do not know.

> This cocoa is very hot. —How hot is it? It is very hot. Can you drink it? We do not know.

> This cocoa is too hot. How hot is it? It is too hot. Can you drink it? No. You will have to wait for it to cool.

Your Adverbs Have Adverbs!

Some adverbs even modify other adverbs:

> Freda arrived too late.

When did Freda arrive? The adverb *late* tells when Freda arrived. *Too* tells to what extent she was late. *Too* is an adverb that modifies the adverb *late.*

> Jane almost never oversleeps.

The adverb *never* tells when Jane oversleeps. *Almost* tells to what extent. *Almost* is an adverb that modifies the adverb *never.*

BRAIN GAMES

Adverbs of Frequency

How often do you make your bed? Always? Sometimes? Never? Adverbs that tell how often something happens are called *adverbs of frequency*. The adverbs *always, usually, often, sometimes, seldom, rarely, never* are hidden in the word-search puzzle. Find and circle them.

Word-Search Puzzle

Z	N	G	W	U	S	U	A	L	L	Y	T	S
A	D	H	J	I	U	R	A	R	E	L	Y	U
U	A	N	I	M	E	M	O	U	Z	L	K	T
K	W	H	E	V	H	N	C	P	D	T	A	Z
B	Y	K	E	T	X	S	E	L	D	O	M	C
E	S	N	E	T	F	O	T	F	Y	B	S	P
R	W	I	C	D	U	M	L	Y	G	E	C	T
A	O	T	F	R	A	E	Z	D	M	L	X	R
F	L	S	E	W	H	T	Q	K	M	V	D	O
N	Q	W	C	O	T	I	W	B	O	I	H	V
M	E	D	A	B	F	M	A	A	S	P	T	F
Q	N	C	T	Y	E	E	H	R	L	C	Y	W
O	S	S	X	V	S	S	W	R	F	D	J	I

Answers are on page 97.

Where Does an Adverb Go?

Think about adjectives again. Where do they go in a sentence? They are almost always placed beside the noun or pronoun they tell about (a *sunburned* zebra, a *dancing* alligator). Adverbs, on the other hand, get to wander around more. When an adverb tells about a verb, it often can go in more than one place in a sentence—and still make sense. Watch the moving adverb in this sentence:

The storm will end soon.
The storm will soon end.
Soon, the storm will end.

What about adverbs that modify an adjective or another adverb? These usually come right before the word they modify. You might say these adverbs are on a short leash!

The rain was quite heavy.
It almost never rains this heavily.

The word *not* is an adverb. So is the contraction *-n't*. Notice that *not* comes between a helping verb and a main verb.

I do not like to carry my umbrella.
As a result, it can't keep me dry!

Adverb or Adjective: Which Should You Use?

Kim plays awesome violin. To compliment her, should you say "You play wonderful" or "You play wonderfully"? The last sentence is correct. Let's take a closer look at adjectives and adverbs.

QUESTIONS AND ANSWERS

As a writer, you want to use adverbs and adjectives. They make your sentences more interesting. But how do you know whether to use an adverb or an adjective? Ask yourself this question: What word is being modified?

The drummer beat _____ on the timpani drum. (loud, loudly)

What word in the sentence is being modified? The verb *beat* is being modified. How did the drummer beat on the drum? Only an adverb can modify a verb, so *loudly* is the correct word.

Listening to the orchestra,
soon I was _____.
(happy, happily)

What word in the sentence is being modified? Notice that the linking verb *was* links the subject *I* to a predicate word. The predicate word describes the subject. Only adjectives can describe nouns and pronouns, so the predicate word must be an adjective. *Happy* is the correct word.

CHECKUP ✔

Ride the Roller Coaster!

Ask yourself which word is being modified. Do you need an adjective or an adverb? Write the correct word in the blank.

1. Katie and I rode the roller coaster _____. (happy, happily)

2. But Mom was _____ the whole time. (nervous, nervously)

3. The coaster chugged _____ up the first hill. (slow, slowly)

4. Then it flew _____ down the other side. (swift, swiftly)

5. Mom screamed _____. (loud, loudly)

6. "That was _____ fun!" Mom said. "Let's go again!" (great, greatly)

Answers are on page 97.

GOOD/WELL VS. BAD/BADLY

Do you play sports *good* or *well*? Does your onion ice cream taste *bad* or *badly*? These pairs of words confuse everyone! Knowing which is an adjective and which is an adverb will help you use them correctly.

Good is an adjective. It modifies nouns and pronouns. *Well* is an adverb. It tells how something is done.

> That was a good throw. (adjective)

> You look good in that uniform! (adjective after linking verb)

> You threw the ball well today. (adverb)

Well is also used as an adjective that means "in good health."

> Don't you feel well? (adjective after linking verb)

To see if *well* is used as an adjective or adverb, ask what question it answers. Does it tell how an action was done? Then it is an adverb. Does it describe a person's health? Then it is an adjective.

Slipups
I Feel Good

Feel good and *feel well* mean different things.

> *Feel good* means "to feel happy or pleased."
>> I feel good about our chances this season.

> *Feel well* means "to feel healthy."
>> I feel well enough to play.

It's a good idea to stop and think about what you feel before you write *good* or *well*. Remember, use *well* to describe your health.

Bad is an adjective. Therefore, it should be used after a linking verb. The adverb *badly* should be used with an action verb.

"I am a bad player," said Teddy. (adjective)
"Don't feel bad," said Freddy. (adjective after helping verb)
"The pitcher is throwing badly," said the coach. (adverb after action verb)

BRAIN GAMES

The Good, the Bad, and the Squirrelly

What does each sentence need? An adjective or an adverb? Write *good*, *well*, *bad*, or *badly* to complete each sentence.

1. It was a _____ day for the game. (good, well)

2. The Squirrels and the Cubs both hoped they would play _____. (good, well)

3. Sammy Squirrel was nervous and said he did not feel _____. (good, well)

4. "Relax, Sammy," said Coach. "I know you had a _____ practice." (bad, badly)

5. "You are a very _____ pitcher," he said. (good, well)

6. Sammy did not pitch _____ at all. (bad, badly)

Answers are on page 97.

CHECKUP ✓

Superheroes

Read the following sentences. Write down if the underlined word is an adjective or an adverb.

1. Superman <u>usually</u> wins the contest for favorite superhero.
2. However, many kids think Spider-Man is <u>cool</u>, too.
3. Superman is <u>incredibly</u> strong, and he can fly!
4. With spider abilities, Spider-Man climbs <u>easily</u> up tall buildings.
5. With fewer super strengths than Superman, he must be more <u>clever</u>.

Now write a sentence about your favorite superhero. Use at least one adjective and one adverb!

Answers are on page 97.

Adverbs that Compare

FORMS OF COMPARISON

Remember that adjectives have different forms to compare.

A bright green would look good on this tree house. (positive form)
This green is brighter than that green. (comparative form)
That is the brightest green paint I have ever seen! (superlative form)

Adverbs also have comparative and superlative forms. The *comparative form* of an adverb compares two actions. The *superlative form* compares three or more actions.

ENDINGS -ER AND -EST

Many short adverbs form the comparative form by adding -er to the end. They form the superlative form by adding -est.

Positive	Comparative	Superlative
hard	harder	hardest
fast	faster	fastest
late	later	latest
soon	sooner	soonest
early	earlier	earliest

The carpenters worked hard.
The roofers worked harder.
The painters worked hardest
  of all.

MORE AND MOST

Longer adverbs and adverbs
ending in -ly form the
comparative by adding the word
more. They form the superlative
by adding the word most.

Positive	Comparative	Superlative
quickly	more quickly	most quickly
carefully	more carefully	most carefully
happily	more happily	most happily

The walls went up quickly.
The roof was finished more quickly than the walls.
The painting was completed most quickly of all.

IRREGULAR FORMS

You know the rule in English grammar: Every rule has exceptions! So does the
rule for the forms of comparison. Some adverbs have totally different words for
the comparative and superlative forms.

Positive	Comparative	Superlative
well	better	best
badly	worse	worst
little	less	least
much	more	most
far	farther	farthest

One paintbrush works well.
Two paintbrushes work better.
Two paintbrushes and a tail work best of all.

BRAIN GAMES

Crossword of Comparison

All these answers have to do with adverbs of comparison.

ACROSS

3. comparative form of *well*
4. superlative form of *early*
8. The base form of the adverb
   is the _____ form.
9. superlative form of *far*
10. _____, worse, worst
11. comparative form of *high*

DOWN

1. superlative form of *happily*
2. comparative form of *quickly*
5. adverb form that uses –*est*
6. little, less, _____
7. superlative form of *much*

Answers are on page 97.

Double Negatives

Two wrongs don't make a right. Neither do two negatives. A negative is a word that means "no." You should only use one negative in a sentence. Using two negatives in a sentence causes a mistake called a *double negative*.

> **Detective:** All right! You might as well tell me
>   what you know.
> **Suspect:** I don't know nothing.
> **Detective:** Aha! So you admit you know
>   something!

What did the suspect mean to say? Words that mean *not* are tricky!

DOUBLE TROUBLE

Here is a list of negatives:

no	no one	hardly
not (n't)	nobody	barely
none	nothing	scarcely
nowhere	never	

Notice that many of the negatives have the word *no* in them. The contraction *n't* is a negative because it stands for *not*. Other words in the list have a negative meaning, though they do not have the word *no* in them.

I don't have no trouble with English. (two negatives)

To correct a double negative, change one negative word to a positive word. Or, sometimes you can just remove one negative word.

I don't have any trouble with English. (one negative)
I have no trouble with English. (one negative)

Answers

page 87

ADVERB SORT
How? bravely, slowly, carefully, excitedly
When? yesterday, never
Where? up
To What Extent? extremely, terribly finally, almost

page 88

VERY PUNNY
flatly, tartly, dryly, coldly, breezily

page 90

ADVERBS OF FREQUENCY

```
Z N G W U S U A L L Y T S
A D H J I U R A R E L Y U
U A N I M E M O U Z L K T
K W H E V H N C P D T A Z
B Y K E T X S E L D O M C
E S N E T F O T F Y B S P
R W I C D U M L Y G E C T
A O T F R A E Z D M L X R
F L S E W H T Q K M V D O
N Q W C O T I W B O I H V
M E D A B F M A A S P T F
Q N C T Y E E H R L C Y W
O S S X V S S W R F D J I
```

page 92

CHECKUP
1) happily; 2) nervous; 3) slowly;
4) swiftly; 5) loudly; 6) great

page 93

THE GOOD, THE BAD, AND THE SQUIRRELLY
1) good; 2) well; 3) well; 4) bad;
5) good; 6) badly

page 94

CHECKUP
1) adverb; 2) adjective; 3) adverb;
4) adverb; 5) adjective

page 96

CROSSWORD OF COMPARISON

ACROSS	DOWN
3. better	1. most happily
4. earliest	2. more quickly
8. positive	5. superlative
9. farthest	6. least
10. badly	7. most
11. higher	

Prepositions, Conjunctions, and Interjections
Words That Relate, Connect, and Show Feeling

Mom: "Put on your shoes, please."
Kid: "Which ones? The shoes in the closet?
The ones under the bed? The ones beside the door?"

What Is a Preposition?

A *preposition* shows a relationship between words in a sentence. Suppose you want to tell someone about watching cooks make pancakes for breakfast. You may say,

> A cook held a spatula above the griddle. Another cook slid a spatula under a pancake to turn it. The pancakes are on the griddle.

The words *above, under,* and *on* show where each thing is in relation to something else—they are prepositions.

Here are other examples of using prepositions in sentences:

> The cat likes to hide behind the chair. Sometimes she sits beneath the table and jumps on your lap.

Prepositions show the relationship of a noun or pronoun to another word in the sentence. The noun or pronoun comes after the preposition and is called the *object of the preposition.*

> The dog ran around the tree.

In this example, the preposition *around* shows the relationship between the noun *tree* and the noun *dog.* If you change the preposition, the relationship changes. What if the dog was *in* the tree or *under* the tree?

Here is a list of common prepositions.

Common Prepositions

about	beneath	inside	since
above	beside	into	through
across	between	like	throughout
after	beyond	near	to
against	but	of	toward
along	by	off	under
among	down	on	underneath
around	during	onto	until
at	except	out	up
before	for	outside	upon
behind	from	over	with
below	in	past	without

Pick the Preposition

At the end of each sentence, you'll see a choice of prepositions in parentheses. Circle the preposition that best shows the relationship.

1. Did you see the movie _____ TV last night? (in/on)

2. It was a sci-fi thriller ____ life on Mars. (about/until)

3. Some humans traveled _____ the planet ____ a spaceship. (at/to, behind/inside)

4. They crashed ____ the surface. (onto/under)

5. They saw no signs ____ life anywhere ____ them. (for/of, around/toward)

6. A red desert stretched ____ them. (before/off)

7. They saw mountains ____ the distance. (at/in)

8. They began the long walk _____ the desert. (across/down)

9. Little did they know they were being watched ____ Martians! (by/with)

10. These Martians lived ____ the surface to escape extreme temperatures ____ hot and cold. (between/under, of/over)

Answers are on page 114.

Tricks

A preposition is always followed by a noun or a pronoun. It is never followed by a verb.

Do not eat sweets **before** supper. —*Before* is a preposition; *supper* is a noun.

In, On, At

The prepositions *in*, *on*, and *at* are easy to confuse. All three can be used to relate where and when.

HOW DO YOU TELL SOMEONE WHERE YOU LIVE?

Use *in* to describe large areas such as countries or states.

> I live in Illinois.

Use *on* to describe the street name.

> I live on Bethany Road.

Use *at* to give the exact numbered address.

> I live at 9234 Bethany Road.

HOW DO YOU TELL WHEN SOMETHING HAPPENED?

Use *in* to give a period of time, a year, a season, or a month.

> We started school in late summer.

Use *on* to tell a specific day.

> We started school on August 21.

Use *at* to tell the specific time.

> We started school at 8:00 A.M.

FUN FACT
In the Top Ten

There are only about 150 prepositions in English, but they are important words. In fact, the prepositions *of, to,* and *in* rank in the top ten. They are among the most often used words in English!

BRAIN GAMES

Idioms Crossword

Idioms are everyday sayings that don't make sense if you think about what each word means. What prepositions are missing from these idioms? Once you complete the puzzle, get together with friends. Talk about what you think the idioms mean.

ACROSS

2. Run ____ the first sign of trouble.

4. That goes ____ the grain.

5. ____ the blue horizon

6. _____ the top

7. I'm really ____ the eight ball now.

DOWN

1. We've run ____ of luck.

2. I ran ____ some old photos.

3. It went off ____ a hitch.

5. That silly behavior is ____ my dignity.

Answers are on page 114.

Prepositional Phrases

Where you find a preposition, you will find a prepositional phrase. A *prepositional phrase* is a group of words that begins with a preposition and has an object of the preposition. The *object of the preposition* may be a noun or pronoun. In the example below, *to* is the preposition and the pronoun *me* is the object of the preposition.

Jane threw the ball to me.

A prepositional phrase often contains adjectives, too. In the next example, *into* is the preposition and the noun *sky* is the object of the preposition. The adjectives *clear* and *blue* describe the object of the preposition. They are part of the prepositional phrase.

> The kite sailed into the clear blue sky.

This sentence has three prepositional phrases in a row.

> I will meet you beside the pond in the park on Friday.

Tricks

In Front—A Preposition

The word *preposition* means "to be placed in front of." This can help you remember that a preposition is always the first word in a prepositional phrase.

What part of the sentence above is most important? All of it! Take away any of the phrases after the word *you*, and the reader will not know the answers to the questions *where* or *when*.

CHECKUP ✔

Picture It with Prepositions

Use the prepositional phrases in the word bank to finish the story.

Word Bank

like a rag doll	into the air	from her
for Frogins and the ducks	in the park	for him
with brown spots	with his teeth	after it
over his shoulder	before him	

Jane and her dog Frogins play Frisbee™ _____. Frogins is a cute white dog _____. He is also a great catcher. He can leap _____ higher than my head. He grabs the flying disk _____. Then the game begins! He shakes it _____. When Jane tries to take it, he runs away _____. "Catch me if you can!" he seems to say. This is great fun _____! One day Jane threw the disk very far. Frogins ran _____ in a blur. He looked _____ for it. He didn't see the pond _____. Splash! What a surprise _____!

Answers are on page 114.

Pronouns After Prepositions—For Me?

Remember that the object of a preposition can be a pronoun. But here's a tricky part: Not all pronouns can be the object of a preposition. Do you know why? Let's take time for a short review of pronouns.

Some personal pronouns are used as subjects. Some can be used only as objects. *Subject pronouns* are used as subjects or after linking verbs. *Object pronouns* are used as objects of verbs or objects of prepositions.

Subject Pronouns	Object Pronouns
I	me
you	you
he	him
she	her
it	it
we	us
they	them

You know you should use *I* and other subject pronouns as subjects. It wouldn't sound right to say "*Me* like this game" or "*Us* have the same jacket." It does sound right to say "*I* like this game" and "*We* have the same jacket." But you have less practice at how object pronouns should sound. Which of these sentences uses the correct prepositional phrase?

> I have a ticket for he and I.
> I have a ticket for him and me.

For is a preposition and object pronouns must be used with it. The second sentence is correct:

> I have a ticket for him and me.

Study these sentences. They show correct use of pronouns with prepositions.

> Anna went to the game with me.
> Dad bought team pennants for us.
> We sat beside him.
> Oops! I spilled my water on her.
> Fans asked the game's hero to sign autographs for them.

This isn't too hard, is it? Where it gets confusing is when there are two objects of the preposition. Sometimes a noun and a pronoun are used as the objects of the same preposition.

Seeing the game was fun for Dad and _____. (us, we)

What pronoun do you use? "for Dad and us" is correct. Remember, prepositions take object pronouns.

Tricks

Try reading the sentence with only the pronoun after the preposition.

Seeing the game was fun for Dad and _____ (I/me).
Seeing the game was fun for _____ (I/me).

The object pronoun *me* is the correct choice for both.

How Are Your Phrases Acting?

Just as nouns and verbs have jobs, phrases have jobs, too. Prepositional phrases act like adjectives and adverbs because they modify other words.

ADJECTIVE PHRASES

An adjective modifies a noun or pronoun. It tells *what kind, which one,* or *how many*. A prepositional phrase can also modify a noun or pronoun. It is called an *adjective phrase*. An adjective phrase tells *what kind* or *which one*.

Adjective before a noun: That is an exciting play.
Noun with an adjective phrase: It is a play with suspense and laughs.

What kind of play is it? An *exciting* play. A play *with suspense and laughs*. Both the adjective and the adjective phrase modify the noun *play*.

Adjective before a noun: Bring that prop.
Noun with an adjective phrase: Bring the prop on the top shelf.

Which prop should you bring? *That* prop. The prop *on the top shelf.* The adjective and the adjective phrase modify the noun *prop.*

ADVERB PHRASES

An adverb modifies a verb, an adjective, or another adverb. It tells *how, where, when,* or *to what extent.* A prepositional phrase can act as an adverb. It is called an *adverb phrase.* An adverb phrase tells *how, when, where,* or *to what extent.*

> Verb with an adverb: We rehearse often.
> Verb with an adverb phrase: We rehearse on Saturdays.

> Verb with an adverb: We rehearse here.
> Verb with an adverb phrase: We rehearse at my house.

Adverb phrases can modify adjectives and other adverbs, too.

> Adjective with an adverb phrase: This play is fun for us.
> Adverb with an adverb phrase: You act well for a beginner.

The adverb phrase *for us* modifies the adjective *fun.* The adverb phrase *for a beginner* modifies the adverb *well.*

BRAIN GAMES

Are You in the Scene?

Use an adjective phrase or adverb phrase from the list to complete each sentence.

Adjective Phrases	Adverb Phrases
of strategy	after the discovery
in the mountains	on horses
with them	

1. The movie actors had to learn to twirl a rope as they rode _____.

2. As they wait for their next scene, the actors play checkers, a game _____.

3. This movie is about cowhands who discover a lost gold mine _____.

4. The cowhands do not change _____.

5. The last scene ends _____ still on the ranch.

Answers are on page 114.

BRAIN GAMES

Phrases from Famous Americans

Benjamin Franklin was a printer, an inventor, and a diplomat. President Abraham Lincoln was the 16th president of the United States. Helen Keller overcame blindness and deafness to become a great communicator. Look at their words. Underline each prepositional phrase. Write whether it is an *adjective phrase* or *adverb phrase*.

1. Benjamin Franklin: "Whatever is begun in anger ends in shame."

2. Abraham Lincoln: "The best thing about the future is that it comes one day at a time."

3. Helen Keller: "The best and most beautiful things in the world cannot be seen or even touched. They must be felt with the heart."

Answers are on page 114.

Put Phrases in Their Place

Be careful where you put prepositional phrases.

In the soup Sherry put the bread.

You might ask what Sherry was doing in the soup. Sure, you know Sherry added bread to her soup. But that's not what the sentence says. It says that Sherry was in the soup. To make your sentences clear, put the prepositional phrase close to the word it modifies.

Sherry put the bread in the soup.

CHECKUP ✔

Headline Bloopers

Do these headlines turn your head? Rewrite them so they say the right thing. Put the phrases in the right place.

1. Dog Scares Letter Carrier with No Collar
2. Girl Finds Postcards Written by Grandparents in Attic
3. Patients Laugh at Clowns in Hospital

Answers are on page 114.

Can an Adverb Change Its Spots?

The word *above* is a preposition. All by itself it tells where, so that makes it an adverb. But what if it has a noun as an object? Then it is a preposition.

> A gull hovered above.
> A gull hovered above the snack bar.

Some words from our preposition list can be used as either adverbs or prepositions. They are:

above	by	over
inside	outside	around
in	out	
up	down	

When used as prepositions, these words have nouns or pronouns as objects. For example, look at the words *around* and *over* in the following sentences.

> The swimmers looked around and swam over.
> The swimmers looked around the reef and swam over the coral.

In the first sentence, *around* and *over* are adverbs. They do not have nouns or pronouns as their objects. In the second sentence, *around* and *over* are prepositions. They do have nouns as their objects.

Conjunctions—The Joiners

Bob likes comedies. Joy likes comedies. Bob likes games. Joy likes games.

Help! This writing is boring because it repeats itself. What word can come to the rescue here? The useful word *and*!

Bob and Joy like comedies and games.

Conjunctions are words that join. A conjunction may join two words, two phrases, or two sentences.

Ling likes movies and music.
—Conjunction *and* joins two words.

The music store is open now but will soon close. —Conjunction *but* joins two verb phrases.

We stop there every week although we seldom rent anything.
—Conjunction *although* joins two sentences.

There are three kinds of conjunctions to do three kinds of jobs: workhorse conjunctions, conjunctions in pairs, and conjunctions with clauses.

WORKHORSE CONJUNCTIONS

The most common conjunctions—*and, but, or, for, nor, so, yet*—are workhorses because we need to use them often to make compounds.

The following sentences show how the conjunction makes a compound subject:

Tim went to the farmers' market. Angelina went to the farmers' market. Tim and Angelina went to the farmers' market.

These sentences show how the conjunction makes a compound object:

At the market, Tim met a baker. He also met a farmer.
At the market, Tim met a baker and a farmer.

What if three or more sentence parts are joined? Put commas between each item. Then put the conjunction before the last item. This compound object has three parts:

You can make juice, sauce, or jelly from apples.

A conjunction can join whole sentences to make a compound sentence. (Put a comma before the conjunction when you join them.)

The farmer wanted to buy lemons. The baker wanted to get apples.
The farmer wanted lemons, but the baker wanted to buy apples.

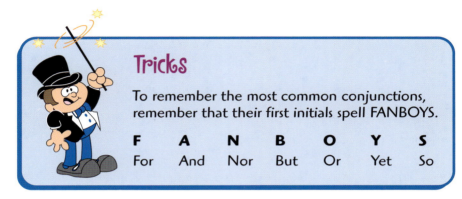

Tricks

To remember the most common conjunctions, remember that their first initials spell FANBOYS.

F	A	N	B	O	Y	S
For	And	Nor	But	Or	Yet	So

CHECKUP ✔

Putting It Together

Use one of the common conjunctions to combine each pair of sentences. Write your new sentences.

1. Apples are crisp. They are also delicious.

2. The farmer grows apples. He also picks them.

3. The farmer puts the apples in baskets. Other apples go in boxes.

4. Bruised apples go to the press. They can be made into cider.

5. The work is tiring. It is also fun.

Answers are on page 115.

CONJUNCTION PAIRS

Some conjunctions come in pairs. They work together as partners to join words or groups of words.

both...and neither...nor
either...or not only...but also

These examples show how conjunction pairs join sentence parts.

Both Jean and Paula went to the cafeteria. —Conjunction pair joins subjects.

I will go with either Matt or John. —Conjunction pair joins objects.

The students neither know nor care about how the food is prepared. —Conjunction pair joins verbs.

The food was not only tasty but also healthy. —Conjunction pair joins adjectives.

BRAIN GAMES

Pairs of Pears

Find the conjunction pair in each sentence. Circle both partners.

1. Kelly said that the pear was not only hard but also bitter.
2. Either it was not ripe, or her taste buds were off.
3. A ripe pear is not only sweet but also juicy.
4. Neither the brown nor the green pears get soft as they ripen.
5. Both Kelly and Marie took a bite of the pear.

Answers are on page 115.

CONJUNCTIONS WITH CLAUSES

A third kind of conjunction joins independent clauses and dependent clauses in sentences. A *clause* is a group of words with a subject and a predicate. Every sentence contains at least one clause. It may have more than one. This is where conjunctions come in.

Here is a list of some conjunctions that begin dependent clauses and join them to main clauses:

after	as though	if	until
although	because	since	when
as	before	than	where
as if	even though	unless	while

These conjunctions join clauses in a way that makes one clause depend on the other for meaning. The *dependent clause* cannot stand by itself:

When we go to Washington, D.C.
Until bedtime.
If we can stay awake long enough.

None of the clauses above makes sense alone. You need more information to complete the thought. You must add an independent clause to each dependent clause. The independent clause has a subject and a verb and can stand alone.

When we go to Washington, D.C., we will have the best time.

We can see the Washington Monument and later watch movies until bedtime.

If we can stay awake long enough, we will tell scary stories.

Slipups

A Comma with That Clause?

If the dependent clause comes first in the sentence, put a comma after it. If it comes at the end, you do not need a comma.

When he tells a scary story, Brent turns on a flashlight in the dark.

We always have fun at a sleepover *even though* we don't sleep much.

BRAIN GAMES

Birthday Party

Underline the dependent clause in each sentence. Add a comma if it is needed.

Example: I can't wait for tomorrow <u>because it is my birthday</u>.

1. After school is out my friends are coming over.

2. Although not everyone knows how to bowl we are going bowling.

3. Mom has ordered pizza to be delivered while we are at the bowling alley.

4. When we get home we will have cake and ice cream.

5. Until it is time for bed we will watch movies.

Dad, the Pancake Man

Read and complete the story. Which conjunction fits? Choose the one that shows the relationship between the clauses.

1. We are having pancakes for breakfast _____ they are my favorite. (although, because, unless)

2. Dad makes pancakes _____ he was a chef. (as if, when, while)

3. The first pancake is poured _____ the griddle is the perfect temperature. (after, before, when)

4. He has been making pancakes _____ I was little. (before, since, until)

5. Put butter on your pancakes _____ you pour on syrup. (after, before, while)

Answers are on page 115.

Interjections—Little Words with a Powerful Punch

Shazam! Ouch! Holy cow! Comic book heroes use words like these to express surprise, excitement, pain, or understanding. The words aren't nouns or verbs or modifiers. They don't join anything in a sentence. What do we call these words? *Interjections.* They are words that express strong feeling.

We use them often in speaking. Have you ever used these interjections?

Oh!   Ah!   Well!   Wow!
Oops!   Ouch!   Help!   Hey!

Interjections are usually used with a sentence. Often, they are separated from the sentence by an exclamation point (!). Then the first letter of the first word of the rest of the sentence is capitalized.

Wow! Your new bike is great.

CHECKUP ✔

Buddies on Bikes
Circle the interjections in this story.

"Hey! Where are you going?" asked Brian.

"Ah, I'm just going for a ride," said Zach.

"Well, I could come with you," suggested Brian. "I want to try the new tires on my bike."

Drat! Zach didn't want any company today, but what could he say? "Oh, I guess that will be okay. It's just that it will be boring. Are you sure you want to go?"

Soon the boys were pedaling over a trail on their mountain bikes. Going down a steep hill, Zach hit a sharp rock. Bam! His front tire blew. The bike and Zach went down.

"Ouch! My leg really hurts," said Zach.

"Oh, no! Are you okay?" asked Brian.

Brian was able to ride for help. Zach was glad his buddy had tagged along.

Answers are on page 115.

Answers

page 99

CHECKUP

1. on
2. about
3. to, inside
4. onto
5. of, around
6. before
7. in
8. across
9. by
10. under, of

page 101

IDIOMS CROSSWORD

ACROSS
2. at
4. against
5. beyond
6. over
7. behind

DOWN
1. out
2. across
3. without
5. beneath

page 102

CHECKUP

Jane and her dog Frogins play Frisbee™ in the park. Frogins is a cute white dog with brown spots. He is also a great catcher. He can leap into the air higher than my head. He grabs the flying disk with his teeth. Then the game begins! He shakes it like a rag doll. When Jane tries to take it, he runs away from her. "Catch me if you can!" he seems to say. This is great fun for him! One day Jane threw the disk very far. Frogins ran after it in a blur. He looked over his shoulder for it. He didn't see the pond before him. Splash! What a surprise for Frogins and the ducks!

page 105

ARE YOU IN THE SCENE?

1. on horses
2. of strategy
3. in the mountains
4. after the discovery
5. with them

page 106

PHRASES FROM FAMOUS AMERICANS

1. in anger, adverb phrase
   in shame, adverb phrase
2. about the future, adjective phrase
   at a time, adjective phrase
3. in the world, adjective phrase
   with the heart, adverb phrase

page 107

CHECKUP

1. Dog with No Collar Scares Letter Carrier
2. In Attic, Girl Finds Postcards Written by Grandparents
3. Patients in Hospital Laugh at Clowns

page 109

CHECKUP

1. Apples are crisp and delicious.
2. The farmer grows and picks apples.
3. The farmer puts the apples in baskets or boxes.
4. Bruised apples go to the press, so they can be made into cider.
5. The work is tiring but fun.

page 110

PAIRS OF PEARS

1. not only...but also
2. Either...or
3. not only...but also
4. Neither...nor
5. Both...and

page 112

BIRTHDAY PARTY

1. After school is out, my friends are coming over.

2. Although not everyone knows how to bowl, we are going bowling.

3. Mom has ordered pizza to be delivered while we are at the bowling alley.

4. When we get home, we will have cake and ice cream.

5. Until it is time for bed, we will watch movies.

DAD, THE PANCAKE MAN

1. because
2. as if
3. when
4. since
5. before

page 113

CHECKUP

Hey!
Ah,
Well,
Drat!
Oh,
Bam!
Ouch!
Oh, no!

Capitalization and Punctuation
The Signs of Communicating

Part of the English language is not words. What is it?
Capital letters and marks of punctuation.

On the road to communication, we count on capitalized letters and punctuation marks (such as periods, question marks, and exclamation points) to help us find our way through even simple messages. The invitation below is missing these important signs. Do you think this makes it harder to read?

please come to a st. patrick's day party at 123 greenway road columbus indiana at 200 p m on saturday march 17 i hope you can help me celebrate

Capital Ideas

In English, proper nouns are capitalized. This means the words begin with capital letters. Nouns name particular people, places, and things. This table shows some proper nouns.

Proper Nouns	Examples
A person's name, initials, and title	Ms. Tameeka Jones Dr. S. B. Lee
Days, months, holidays, historical events (but not seasons)	Monday, June, Fourth of July, World War II, winter

Places:
  Geographic
  Buildings and structures
	
	Africa, Tokyo, Amazon River
	Sears Tower, Golden Gate Bridge, White House

Planets, heavenly bodies	Venus, Milky Way
Businesses, organizations	American Airlines, General Electric, Girl Scouts of America, Food and Drug Administration
Nationalities, languages	Native American, Italian, French
Religious terms	Islam, Jewish, New Testament
First word and important words in titles	*The Phantom Tollbooth* *Sports Illustrated for Kids*
Sections of a country or the world	the South the Eastern Hemisphere

FIRST WORDS

Capitalize the first word of every sentence.

The camping trip was awesome.
Have you ever paddled a canoe?

Capitalize the first word of a *quotation*. A quotation is the repeating of someone's exact words. They are placed inside (" ") marks.

The guide said, "Stay on the marked paths."

If the words *he said* or *she said* come in the middle of the quotation, capitalize the second part only if it starts a new sentence.

"Do you think," I asked, "that we will get some good pictures?"
"Don't worry," he said. "The waterfall along the way is beautiful."

The Rest of the Story

Some special cases call for capitalized letters, too.

Always capitalize the pronoun *I*.

Joe and I will eat the whole bag of popcorn.

Capitalize the greetings and closings in letters.

Dear Mom,   Love, Harry

BRAIN GAMES

A Proper Adventure

Harry wrote this postcard to his aunt. Fix his capitalization mistakes. Cross out lowercase letters that should be capitalized. Write the capital letters above them.

dear aunt louise,

the desert in egypt has sand hills as big as mount everest! our friend dr. tomas serrano went with us from cairo to khartoum. he said, "you must see the great pyramids." he has traveled the world from rome to singapore. we took a trip by camel over the dunes. my camel's name was fahrouk. he was so stubborn he reminded me of uncle dan!

love, harry

Answers are on page 124.

Capital Questions

Some rules of capitalization seem easy but can cause confusion.

TITLES

A title is a proper noun. It can have many words. Do you capitalize all the words in the title?

The rule says to capitalize the first word and all "important" words in a title. It's easier to do if you know which words NOT to capitalize. Do not capitalize *a*, *an*, or *the* unless it is the first word of the title. Do not capitalize short conjunctions (such as *and*, *or*) or short prepositions (such as *in*, *for*, *with*). But always capitalize a verb or helping verb, even if it is very short (such as *is*, *am*). This title shows correctly capitalized letters:

If Life Is a Bowl of Cherries, What Am I Doing in the Pits?

FAMILY RELATIONSHIPS

Many people get confused about when to capitalize *dad*, *mom*, *grandmother*, and other family names. The rule says to capitalize them when they are used as names of specific people. Again, it might be easier to remember when NOT to capitalize. Do not capitalize these words if they follow *a*, *an*, or *the* or a possessive adjective such as *her*, *his*, or *my*.

Tricks

All in the Family

Capitalize words that name family members only when they are used as names.

Thanks for the gift, Uncle Bill.

Get Grandpa to tell you about his childhood.

You will like my aunt.

Tom asked Mom and Grandpa to write family histories.

What did your mom write about her childhood?

A grandparent spoils children more than a father or a mother.

NORTH, SOUTH, EAST, WEST

When the words *north*, *south*, *east*, *west* are used as directions, they are not capitalized.

Go west on Route 66.

When these same words are used to name regions, they are capitalized.

She lives on the East Coast, but she wants to move to the South.

CHECKUP ✔

Great-Grandpa's Story

Fix the mistakes in capitalization. If a sentence is correct, put a star beside it.

1. My mom asked great-grandpa Otis to write about his life.
2. As a young man, he traveled north and west to the Dakotas.
3. It wasn't the wild west, but cowboys were still needed.
4. Uncle Don was born in a little town west of Mitchell, South Dakota.
5. My great-grandpa called his story "my life and times on the dakota plains."

Answers are on page 124.

Punctuation Road Signs

What kind of signal says "Stop here"? What kind says, "Slow down"? What kind says, "Look at the connection between these two"? What kind says, "Allow me to introduce . . ."? Punctuation marks signal all these messages and more to readers.

PERIOD, QUESTION MARK, EXCLAMATION POINT

Sentences end with one of three punctuation marks: a period, a question mark, or an exclamation point. These end marks tell us, "This is the end of a sentence."

End a statement or a mild command with a period (.).

This sandwich needs something extra. Please pass the pickles.

Also use periods after abbreviations. An abbreviation is a shortened form of a word.

St. (Street)   Dr. (Doctor)   Oct. (October)   hr. (hour)

Exceptions: Metric abbreviations do not use periods. Neither do state abbreviations used with ZIP codes on envelopes.

km (kilometer)   ml (milliliter)   GA (Georgia)   NJ (New Jersey)

End a question with a question mark (?).

What is your favorite sandwich?

End a sentence that shows strong feeling with an exclamation point (!).

I dropped my sandwich!

BRAIN GAMES

World's Biggest Salad

Add periods, question marks, and exclamation points where they are needed.

1. *The Guinness Book of World Records* is our favorite book
2. It gives records such as the world's tallest, shortest, or fastest people
3. The record might be in kilograms (kg) or pounds (lb)
4. Do you know what R C Higgins and I decided to do
5. We are going to make the biggest salad ever seen
6. Wow This is so exciting
7. Every kid at Lincoln St School will help
8. Could we use the roller rink on First Avenue as a salad bowl
9. Look out The tomatoes are falling
10. This might be the world's biggest mess

Answers are on page 124.

COMMA: COULD YOU PLEASE SLOW DOWN?

Think of punctuation as a traffic light on the road of communication. If a period is a red light, then a comma is a yellow light. A *comma* signals the reader to pause. Commas are useful because often you need a pause within a sentence.

Commas are used to *separate items in a series.* When you list three or more items in a sentence, put a comma between each item on the list.

Most people like cats, dogs, and fish as pets.
A dog needs room for exercise, time to play, and attention from you.

Commas are used in compound sentences to *separate the sentences.* The comma is placed before the conjunctions *and, but, or.* The conjunction shows the two thoughts are connected. The comma signals the pause between the thoughts.

> Dogs need to go outdoors often, but cats can be happy living indoors.
> Parakeets can talk, and they can also learn tricks.

Commas are used to *set off extra words in a sentence.* We often add words to a basic sentence. Because the words are not needed to understand the sentence, they are set off by a comma. Sometimes they are words at the front or back of a sentence.

> Come here, Patches! Carl, have you seen the leash?
> Oh, we need to take dog treats, too.

Sometimes the extra words are groups of words inside a sentence. They modify words in the sentence or explain something. Added phrases and clauses like these are set off by commas.

> Shep, a Border collie, is a smart dog.
> Shep's trainer, who works with world champions, is a wizard with dogs.

CONVENTIONAL USES OF COMMAS
The word *conventional* means we agree to use commas in these cases. The commas do not indicate a pause, but they help make the meaning clear.

DATES
In a date, put a comma before the year.

> The show is August 12, 2004.

ADDRESSES
Use commas to separate the parts of an address. Use a comma between a city and state and between a state or province and country.

> Nashville, Tennessee   Ontario, Canada

For an address in a sentence, use commas between the parts except between the state and ZIP code.

> Write to Seattle Space Needle,
> 219 Fourth Avenue N., Seattle, WA 98109.

LETTERS

Place a comma after the greeting of a personal letter.

Dear Gus,

Place a comma after the closing of a personal or business letter.

Love,   Sincerely yours,

QUOTATIONS

Use commas to set off the speaker's tags *(he said, she said)* from the speaker's words.

"Let's go to the pet store," said Kelly.
Jaimie asked, "What do you want to buy?"
"I'm not sure," she said, "but I might get a fish for my aquarium."

BRAIN GAMES

Pet Parade

In each sentence, add commas where they are needed.
The number of commas needed is shown in parentheses.

1. Inez asked "Ben are you bringing a pet to the pet fair?" (two)
2. "I will bring my fish my gerbils and my rabbit" Ben replied. (three)
3. The fair is at 9:00 A.M. on May 21 2004. (one)
4. The school has rented the gym at 708 Lincoln St. Garden City New York. (two)
5. Martha Hannon our school principal will be the judge. (two)
6. George Hieratos who runs George's Pet Store will give a talk on pet care. (two)

Answers are on page 124.

SEMICOLON, THE SUPERCOMMA!

A semicolon looks like a period on top of a comma. Use a *semicolon* to join two sentences that have a strong connection. You could say that one semicolon is equal to a comma and conjunction (see the second sentence below).

The Smiths are on vacation; I'm dog sitting for them.
OR The Smiths are on vacation, so I'm dog sitting for them.

COLON

A colon looks like two periods stacked.
Use a *colon* to introduce a list or words
that illustrate or explain.

> Paws has three things on her mind: going outside, food, and attention.

> The Smiths also asked me to do the following things: bring in the mail and water the plants.

Colons are also used in exact times and in the greeting of a business letter.

> at 10:30 A.M.   Dear sir:

APOSTROPHE

An apostrophe looks like a comma that floated above the line. An *apostrophe*
signals ownership or contracted words.

> Bill's ferret   the ferret's cage
>
> do not—don't   you are—you're   it is—it's

HYPHEN

A hyphen looks like a minus sign, but it doesn't subtract—it divides! Use
hyphens to divide words at the end of lines. Always divide a word between
syllables. This makes the divided word easier to read. (Do not divide a one-
syllable word!)

> The dog tried to es-
> cape from its kennel.

Hyphens can also connect words.

> That cat knocked twenty-one vases off a shelf!
> Her yellow-green eyes looked innocently at me.

QUOTATION MARKS

In a story, the quotation marks (" ") show when someone is speaking. Use
quotation marks around the words someone says.

> Mike's mom asked, "Did you forget to feed Bandit?"
> "Yeah," Mike replied. "This cat care is harder than it looks."

See page 122 for information about using commas with quotation marks.

Answers

page 117

A PROPER ADVENTURE

Dear Aunt Louise,
The desert in Egypt has sand hills as big as Mount Everest! Our friend Dr. Tomas Serrano went with us from Cairo to Khartoum. He said, "You must see the Great Pyramids." He has traveled the world from Rome to Singapore. We took a trip by camel over the dunes. My camel's name was Fahrouk. He was so stubborn he reminded me of Uncle Dan! Love, Harry

page 119

CHECKUP

1. Great-Grandpa
2. ★
3. Wild West
4. ★
5. "My Life and Times on the Dakota Plains."

page 120

WORLD'S BIGGEST SALAD

1. *The Guinness Book of World Records* is our favorite book.
2. It gives records such as world's tallest, shortest, or fastest people.
3. The record might be in kilograms (kg) or pounds (lb).
4. Do you know what R.C. Higgins and I decided to do?
5. We are going to make the biggest salad ever seen.
6. Wow! This is so exciting!
7. Every kid at Lincoln St. School will help.
8. Could we use the roller rink on First Avenue as a salad bowl?

9. Look out! The tomatoes are falling.
10. This might be the world's biggest mess.

Note: Sometimes one person will consider a sentence to be a statement while another person will consider it to be a sentence with strong feelings. For example, "This might be the world's biggest mess!" (with exclamation point) is how someone, maybe your mom, might say this sentence.

page 122

PET PARADE

1. Inez asked, "Ben, are you bringing a pet to the pet fair?"
2. "I will bring my fish, my gerbils, and my rabbit," Ben replied.
3. The fair is at 9:00 A.M. on May 21, 2004.
4. The school has rented the gym at 708 Lincoln St., Garden City, New York.
5. Martha Hannon, our school principal, will be the judge.
6. George Hieratos, who runs George's Pet Store, will give a talk on pet care.

Index

Index

Index